A SCHOOL CUSTODIAN'S DILEMMA

A School Custodian's Dilemma

Trial By Water And Other Unusual Events

Daniel D. Johnson

authorHOUSE®

AuthorHouse™ LLC
1663 Liberty Drive
Bloomington, IN 47403
www.authorhouse.com
Phone: 1-800-839-8640

Published by AuthorHouse   10/17/2013

ISBN: 978-1-4772-5313-7 (sc)
ISBN: 978-1-4772-5312-0 (e)

Library of Congress Control Number: 2012913487

CONTENTS

Prologue

Something as conspicuous as a coffee spill in the middle of a hallway should garner attention and direct pedestrians to circumnavigate the incident scene. The exception to the rule occurs in a school setting. By the time the driven custodian arrives at the site with wet mop and floor signs, half the puddle transforms into shoe tracks progressing down the hall, fading into oblivion. Once again, the well-intentioned custodian is stupefied.

So who are we? We are the persona of a handyman, janitor, painter, and plumber, assuming dual identity roles. What the average Joe fails to see occurs behind the scenes. We may adopt roles as a public relations representative, referee, occasional counselor, and facility nurse. If need be, we offer a shoulder to cry on. As school employees, we strive to make a difference.

Years ago, on a high school campus built in the middle of a cornfield, a conversation transpired one day between two employees. After sharing a humorous moment, the secretary proposed a suggestion to record events occurring in our high school, for nostalgic purposes. It was an exceptional idea, but I decided to take it to the next level. I created a logbook, which provided an incentive to compose a manuscript, and the wheels were set in motion. Numerous drafts later, a fact-based fictional account of my encounters (from 1992 to 2007) was born.

Life is a perpetual endurance test. This I know. There have been moments when I had to step up to the plate and assert my authority. A battle of wills emerged; challenges were met and then vanquished. The majority of students have been compliant and respectful. Yet, there will always be the handful of inductees into the National Horror Society. Lest we forget, as parents we were once teenagers and assuredly gave our teachers sporadic moments of grief.

Despite life's draconian obstacles, I am reminded of timeless words I have found to be both energizing and motivating. While facing the enemy, Sir Winston Churchill uttered, "Never, never, never give up." I have espoused this motto personally and administered the same to young adults with questionable futures. Only time will determine if the advice I've dispensed was heeded. Wherever your ambitions may take you, continue and do not look back. Doubt feeds procrastination. If that does not persuade you, simply remember the advice of Christian Nestell Bovee: "A failure establishes only this, that our determination to succeed was not strong enough."

In The Beginning

It was impossible to determine what was more hideous, the sight or the putrid smell exuding from the student's locker. The evidence was mounting; it would become one of the most disgusting calls I ever received for a cleanup. Milk cartons were piled high with the contents still inside. What was more disturbing, was the fact that one individual was primarily responsible for all the mayhem.

As the days progressed I was about to discover: it was only the beginning. This occurrence was just the tip of the iceberg for what lay ahead. Anyone who thinks a custodian's duties are restricted to mopping floors, cleaning restrooms, or officiating as a referee in occasional altercations is in for an eye opener. Sometimes I view it as a public relations endeavor, appearing as a diplomat. On other days however, I feel like the students' slave. All I request is simply some respect and nothing more. Is that too much to ask? What I have encountered on the way is challenging, occasionally humbling, and perhaps something right out of the *Twilight Zone*.

That particular spring day greeted me with apprehension when I arrived at the high school. This isn't your typical inner-city brick and mortar compound where the only view is what lies above. No, it is equivalent to a school that has been picked up by a tornado and dropped in the middle of a cornfield, in a valley, somewhere in the Pacific Northwest. No golden arches or taco dive, folks; we are five miles from the nearest burg, surrounded by a sea of pastures and wheat fields. We don't choke on exhaust fumes or listen to the jamming of brake pads. We inhale country odors and hear the utterance of bleating sheep in the distance. If you blink twice when you drive by, you will miss the various sports fields. And by the way, don't sell short the girls' varsity softball team; they're as tough as nails. Legend has it the high school was built on a gravesite, stirring up tales of a night watchman fleeing the property after hearing noises in a restroom. Eerie, but I suspect nomadic arachnids triggering the automatic flushers.

Students of every caliber attend this cornfield palace. From the farmer's sons, to the daughter's of the affluent, they arrive from diverse backgrounds seeking an education. Not everyone will cooperate, however. Out of all the previous attendees, one miscreant has stood out above the rest. So divergent from anyone before or after him, he warranted his own chapter. My apologies readers for not going into detail, but you'll get your fill later. First I need to dish out some personal information.

You're probably wondering about me. How did I, a personable and aspiring individual who once dreamed of a future as an entrepreneur, end up mucking out the boys' room? Evidently, wearing the CEO badge wasn't in the cards, or maybe I was dealt the wrong hand. Granted, there are impediments in every occupation, but I never realized this one would come with a surplus. So why indulge in loathsome cleaning chores? Perhaps it's the zaniness of working with students and the situations they create. Hey, how many executives can claim to have conducted a funeral service on school grounds for a parakeet? That's what I thought. And the day some elementary students learned my first name, they presented me with the pet name "Dan the Flying Man" from the book by the same title. The name stuck until one student in the high school swapped the word "flying" for "janitor." It felt like having my wings clipped.

So here I am, employed at the place of secondary education, but having second thoughts already. Barely two weeks on the job, I arrived home after work one day, moaning and whimpering like a dog that had just been hit by a car.

You have to understand—I had left the miniature splatters of an elementary school, to which I'd become accustomed, and in their place came the mega-spills, food frenzies, and bizarre eating habits reminiscent of the days of *Animal House.* The transition was comparable to trial by fire, or in my case, by water.

The previous custodian, Bob, had decided to hang up his work shoes permanently, and I endeavored to replace them. As the days progressed, the shoes became dead weights, dragging me down like excess baggage. I inherited two items from Bob, and both became more of a curse than a blessing. First, I was presented the traditional set of master keys that would give anyone a feeling of prestige. While desired by many of the staff, no one wanted to bear the burden that was attached. I would be on my cell pleading for a loan if I lost the grandmaster and it fell into the hands of the evil-minded. Add to that the shock of seeing my next paycheck nearly diminished to welfare status.

The other item I simply could not live without was the highly unexpected toilet plunger. How could any custodian function without one, especially at a high school? Analogous to the English bobby and his nightstick, or the soldier and his rifle, the two of us were inseparable as we battled seemingly endless plugged latrines. With just a hint of army boot camp, the repetitious calls became basic training as I emerged from one restroom only to enter yet another. Shirts, shoes, women's thongs, deodorant, photographs, electronics, athletic equipment, and empty cans of chewing tobacco represent a cross section of the items I fished out of the privies.

"Bad day, huh?" commented one family member upon my arrival home one day. Bad is a poor adjective to describe perpetual malfeasance. Sinister is the word that comes to mind. The restrooms, the lunchroom, and the freshman hall, I just wander from one pigsty to another. "They're not like this every day are they?" Pretty much, you have to wonder what the inside of their homes looks like. "ee-yew!".

Gone was the old custodian, somewhere in retirement heaven. Like a new pair of sneakers, it was time for me to be broken in. None of the high school students knew me, so I became the victim of their infrequent epithets. Strolling through the student square one day, I was rendered speechless when one of the female students made a comment about my backside. Was she talking to me? There was no one else in the vicinity. *Excuse me, what did you say?* I thought. What a stark contrast to the elementary school, where the age of innocence still existed. I was as gullible and trusting as an immigrant, fresh off the boat. It was the piercing stares, however, that made me feel like a mannequin just displayed for window dressing.

I was the new kid in town, like a freshman awaiting initiation. I squeezed through crowded hallways, where the walls seemed to be closing in on me. Constantly, I watched over my shoulder for random projectiles. The plunger served dual roles, becoming both a tool and a defensive weapon should the need arise. Surely, it was more than a coincidence that, upon my arrival, the rest rooms were vacated and the stench began to settle in. I discovered yet another toilet deliberately stuffed with paper and a potpourri of forbidden items. This time, however, they did not flush it. Whom should I have thanked?

Drudgery was not restricted to the restrooms. There were other obstacles I met head-on. For some students, jamming lockers had become a daily ritual, and for others, simply remembering their combination was a challenge. Thus was born the locker break-in using the MacGyver technique. Students' memory banks may be younger and more inquisitive, but often they fail to prioritize much-needed information.

Another initiation process was about to unravel. During the summer, the school district had hired a selection of students to assist me in changing locker combinations for the new school year. It seemed like a harmless idea; we would be done in a heartbeat. Fast forward to the first day of school, and we're ready for the rush. Scores of students tried relentlessly to open their lockers without success. Gradually, a long line began to form outside the attendance office. Exasperated and looking for answers, Mrs. Winn, our attendance secretary tried to restrain the mob that had gathered. The conclusion: over one hundred locker combinations were out of sync for the current year, leading to the ritual of resetting each one. That morning sucked. Needless to say, I worked solo the following summer and the results were amazing.

I began learning a deviant language spoken among the students. I discovered graffiti inside lockers and hieroglyphics scrawled on restroom walls. Eventually, I found out which staff members were despised exclusively. Mr. Jones, a stern disciplinarian, heard that his name appeared on a bathroom wall preceded by a profanity and stated, "At least they used the word 'mister.'" Somehow, he saw humor in it, and it failed to provoke him due to the fact that his retirement was imminent. On other days, I went on a mission locating my missing wet floor signs. This is where I learned that the inside of a locker contains naughty hidden secrets. So be careful what you write and where you write it.

Time to get up-close and personal. I would like to present the infamous freshman hallway where these events occur, even as I write. To draw a parallel, envision your trashcan toppled in your front yard, half the contents scattered by the wind and the other half picked over by scavenging blackbirds. Add to that a nauseating odor that culminates after a few days, and the scene is set.

Complaints began pouring in to the high school's main office concerning a smell capable of emptying hallways. Exhaust fumes would have been preferred as retching students fled the scene like queasy carnival riders exiting the Tilt-a-Whirl. At that point, our principal's curiosity was piqued, an investigation ensued, and Sherlock (I wear many hats) was duly summoned.

Coming to a conclusion did not take a rocket scientist. I narrowed it down to one of two lockers with little difficulty. Upon inserting the key, I carefully pulled up on the handle and tested my gag reflexes. Bingo! My search yielded a stack of bloated milk cartons hidden under a sweatshirt, conveniently stored in an unused locker. Right under our noses, this stockpile of spoiled milk had attained the cottage cheese factor. It eluded the staff, including myself. The question arose: how did an empty locker become the recipient of such a collection? To answer this question, I will introduce you to the perpetrator of this incident later. Then you will begin to understand what I had to endure and how our principal, Mr. Rigler, kept his sanity.

The inevitable student prank never ceases to amaze me. While some students are caught, others want to live on the edge and become more brazen. One of the initial pranks I endured brought me to the realization that this secondary facility is in a league of its own. These students have quite the imagination, and, despite ours being a country school, their cognitive abilities never cease to amaze me. On the day of the prank, I was asked to assist some members of the school's Future Farmers of America (FFA) program.

On a placid spring morning, before the halls were bristling with the clamor of locker doors and the buzz of unintelligible student lingo, cattle rustlers arrived. A handful of students decided to remove two heifers from a nearby herd and smuggle them into the high school. On the job only a few short weeks, I was as green as the pasture they were seized from and about to encounter my first escapade. That was the day the radio call from the high school secretary altered my morning routine. She informed me that our pranksters left the poor mooing animals to wander aimlessly up and down the main hall. It was a spectacle watching those little dogies have free run of the building, trying to evade their would-be captor. After what seemed like an eternity, they were finally apprehended, delivered to the capable hands of the FFA, and reunited with the rest of the herd. Eventually, they showed at the county fair and avoided becoming a lunch entrée.

With the cattle gone, I had to deal with the aftermath. There was a *stinkin' mess* left for me in portions that defied the imagination—a smattering of straw and the pungent odor of manure resonated throughout the halls. Bring on the brooms and the scoop shovels. This would become one of my first gross cleanup assignments. The only scene remaining to complete this spectacle was the farmer and his wife standing poised with their pitchforks.

As I said before, this is farm country. Anything can happen, and this was hardly a warm-up for the next event.

In the days before the installation of cameras, specific students took advantage of the situation, doing whatever their scheming minds desired. What you would not see on video would eventually trickle down the grapevine during lunchtime conversation. These were the early stages of progressively unpleasant situations created by only a handful of students. Unfortunately, all it takes is a handful. Perhaps they were frustrated with the establishment. Regardless, I got in the way, and they wanted to see how many buttons they could push. I was vulnerable to just about anything. It was beginning to have all the earmarks of open season on the custodian.

FOOD FRENZY

Stepping into a partially eaten food remnant that has been deliberately compressed for special effect qualifies as one of my pet peeves. The only way to eclipse that annoyance is placing my fingers in chewing gum stuck under a table. Its presence is ubiquitous, unless some savvy administrator issues a decree banning the usage. One day, I accepted the services of student volunteers, who offered to clean under cafeteria tables to minimize a collection that had been accumulating for a year. When the girls concluded their project, they presented me with a softball-sized gum creation. No wonder my putty knife occupies permanent residency in my back pocket. When queried by staff concerning its usage, I simply refer to a minute selection of our cafeteria clientele. The evidence they leave behind is a scene chapter out of *The Haunting*.

Prior to those shenanigans, I recall an incident, known to me as the initiation ceremony, that really caught me off guard. Being the fall guy, I guess it was necessary to pull the rug out from beneath me. Like a private, I was at the bottom of the chain of command. My supervisors (there were many) delivered my paperwork and gave me my orders, and I arrived for duty.

The Gulf War was barely inscribed into the latest history book when an eighteen wheeler bearing "endowments," backed into the loading dock. Wendell, the dock supervisor motioned with his right arm amid the curious eyes of gawking students. Various staff members including administrators, stood shoulder to shoulder, ready to greet the short haul driver. Rudy crawled out of the cab animated, like a little kid with a new toy and informed the district, we were the first to respond. Respond to what? There were no gold bars on the truck, only commodities. The paperwork was signed and the governor gave a thumbs up to a small crowd on hand. All we needed now was a place to store everything.

So, why was everyone excited? "The best things in life are free," or at least that's what the popular song lyrics tell us. If it results in lowering your operating costs or balancing your budget, never refuse a gift from Uncle Sam's kitchen. The administrators saw an opportunity and decided to be dealt into this chance of a lifetime. Just how prominent would these commodities become among the staff and student body? No one really knew at the time; however, one should always expect the unexpected.

Gwendolyn, our food services director, along with district hierarchy, held a powwow on how to get the food program rolling. There was little doubt that Gwendolyn was the Magic Chef. Her resume included "Cook of the Year" honors at the once popular Bourbon Street Steak House. Cooking for the kids was her first love however, and that brought her to the school. She was known to transform a burger patty into a diner's request. The grease pit I emptied verified that. To understand her style, you would need to know this petite but robust lady nicknamed "Grammaw." To the many who assisted her, especially the kitchen helpers, that is who she was. Always caring and compassionate, but also a little wild and crazy on the side. She was not simply the cook, she was the students alter ego. Just don't raise the ire of this little lady. She could crack a mean whip and put those nefarious bad boys in their place.

Case after case, the storeroom was stockpiled with cans of beans, sausages and fish. Those paled in comparison however to the real prized gems containing counterfeit versions of cherry cobbler and chocolate brownies for dessert. Faced with a daunting task, it was up to our kitchen ladies to determine how to present it as palatable to a hypercritical audience. It reminded me of one of the Food Channel's cooking shows. You know, the one that instructs its chef to create an eye-appealing dessert. All the ingredients meld together perfectly until the judges advise the contestants they must use brussels sprouts in the dish. That would kill it for me.

Our kitchen ladies took on the challenge. All the main dishes were heated to food-industry standards, thus avoiding a "Dirty Dining" status. Both staff and students became reluctant recipients of the low-budget delicacy. Everyone was blindsided by the introduction to the new lunch menu. Needing a volunteer (a.k.a. guinea pig), the cooks requisitioned me to sample the cakes and offer my opinion. My initial response was, "Is it possible to improve the taste of cardboard?" I had to give the kitchen staff credit; they were facing a monumental task and a hard sell considering what they had to work with. The lunch became the topic of discussion in the employee lounge overnight. I overheard the comment, "What is this damn stuff anyway?" Perhaps this staff member was a bit judgmental. Some of the staff mused, however, that it must have been a concoction the cooks had dreamed up. They ate it reluctantly.

If memory serves me correctly, the cooks warmed the chocolate cake and then promptly disguised it with a generous layer of cocoa frosting, which gave it a touch of cheap restaurant flair. As droves of hungry high school students crammed the lunch lines, it caught their eye. No one could resist the sight of this mouth-watering treat. Like vultures circling for the kill, they soon caused tray after tray of chocolate cake to disappear, much to the delight of the cooks. Could they repeat the success, they wondered? The top brass met behind closed doors, emerging with a stamp of approval. Everyone's confidence level soared. Grammaw revamped the menu once again on the cooking calendar. Scheduled for the following day for dessert, like a prime time rerun, was chocolate cake.

Word spread throughout the school campus that the reception had been better than anticipated. Eye appeal played a key role in cloaking the contents. As for the school hierarchy, they were living the dream. Discussions arose regarding the acquisition of additional products to build up stock. Like the ever-changing tide, however, requests for the dessert began to recede. Students and staff commenced voicing their opinions and changes in attitude began to evolve. The highly touted main courses were resting permanently on a pallet collecting dust and aging admirably. It appeared the cakes were about to incur the same fate. A revolution was looming.

In an effort to exhaust supply, the kitchen cooks decided to give the desserts celebrity status on the lunch menu. It was a two for one day. Unfortunately, it transpired on the same fateful day that the high school was understaffed. Someone was noticeably missing, perhaps having slipped out early for lunch. The brownies' status plummeted from hero to zero. Whatever the reason, supervision became virtually nonexistent, transforming the cafeteria into the arena of classic food fights. Unsuspecting victims were buffeted with the cakes. For a brief moment, it was bedlam at its finest hour, reminiscent of my high school days. Those sophomores loved to pick on us freshmen and we kept a watchful eye out for half eaten sack lunches launched our direction. Sorry readers, I had to mention the slobs; I get a little sidetracked. With putty knife in hand, I rose to the occasion and began to pry the cakes off the walls, floors and tables. To show their antipathy for the cakes, some students placed them in the classrooms and used them as doorstops. This gave one of our science teachers an opportunity to seize the moment.

Mr. Bauer considered performing a lab analysis on the ingredients to determine weight density. Reminding me of a classic cartoon character, he thoroughly enjoyed his position as science teacher, delving into the world of observation and experimentation. There is one facet of life he enjoyed just as much, lunch. A rotund man in his baby-boomer years, he seldom missed a midday repast. Some days he gave away the extras, particularly desserts. Those holiday lunches brought cheesecake or pumpkin pie topped with whip cream. It was food you would never see again in school. He simply passed it to me. I was the lucky recipient. Ah, the lunches we partook of before the culinary police transformed our eating habits.

A few grumbling students were drafted to assist in the cleanup of this food melee of sizable proportions, and an occasional profanity was overheard. My reaction to their incessant whining was, "Suck it up. You made the mess, so clean it." It was a lesson in humility. Even as the days passed, cakes were found in varying locales, by both staff and the ant populace. That moved us into another phase: pest control. While the upper echelon was baffled at the negative response, most staff was delighted to see the demise of the surplus.

Rumors began circulating that the popularity of Big Brothers bestowal had plummeted among the high school student body like Wall Street in 1987. It was an understatement bar none. For the district's hierarchy, it was sheer disbelief. How was it possible that such a good deal had gone bad? Now it was time for some serious brainstorming.

So what do you do with a gazillion cans of unwanted surplus? You find another recipient. A neighboring high school could be more receptive, so those unsuspecting students became the new beneficiaries. No child would be excluded, and everyone deserved the opportunity to sample it. Well, fool me once, but you cannot fool me twice. Some students at Evergreen Valley High associate with classmates at neighboring Mountain View. They were delighted to pass along a firsthand account of the mutinous affairs in graphic detail. No one wanted to consume the freebies, save the derelicts and the military. The food was adequate on the camp trail, but most students are finicky eaters, especially when it involves school lunches. One day, the surplus simply vanished. The cooks shed no tears, and for the moment, I was as happy as a flea in a kennel.

DUMPSTER DIVING

Some students have a knack for creating their own crisis to attract attention, while others do it simply by accident. A perfect example is a recovery procedure, commonly referred to by staff as "dumpster diving." This occurs when students dispose their food items into the trash along with their lunch tray and student ID card. That's chump change, however, compared to those big-ticket orthodontic retainers that are inadvertently dumped into a 55-gallon trash container. This state of affair evolves into a salvage operation. Reactions vary, as the facial expressions usually paint the grim picture. Among some of the random excuses: "My friend dumped my retainer in the garbage. Do you have any rubber gloves I can use?" "I guess I lost my retainer in the trash . . . again. Could you help me? My mom will kill me if I don't find it!" (When translated, it means no cell phone for a week.) Perhaps a tear will fall, or maybe the panic will begin to materialize. Either way, they come to me, pleading like a first-time offender awaiting trial. That is the moment when the cumbersome green gloves appear, and suddenly I initiate a search-and-rescue mission for all parties involved.

What are the odds of locating a retainer for the same student three times in a school year? A million to one? I should have consulted the odds-makers in Vegas, because one student concluded four rounds of serious excavating. And, I could have pursued it further by contacting the research people at Ripley's. Believe it or not, her retainer was located every time. No, there wasn't a stitch of blond on this girl, but Melissa and I shared a moment of mirth a few years later. This slender redhead with a sense of humor, exhibited her uncanny laugh that was always a head turner. Melissa was a rare specimen indeed, unlike the average female who would have quit after round one.

The success ratio for locating lost orthodontia is likely four to one. How do I know this? Because most students realize the precious plastic is missing from their mouth before the trash is collected. Timing is everything. One day, one of our freshmen girls, Becky, fell into that 25 percent category. She spent nearly an hour in the wretched environment, sifting through mountains of plastic bags. To her chagrin, she was one of those unfortunate students who had waited until I had collected all the trash at the end of the day before notifying me. As everyone in this fast-paced world knows, if you snooze, you lose.

Adolescent teasing by supposedly best friends will not aid the situation, but adds fuel to the fire. "You'll never find it," screamed Ashley and Rachel. "It's buried in the trash can." How is that for a confidence killer? Some words are best left unsaid, and sometimes one only need a bit of encouragement. Our brown-eyed girl appeared underdressed for the occasion, but I solved that problem with a simple wardrobe addition. Becky was outfitted with a pair of gloves, Carhart coveralls and oversized boots that made walking awkward. I provided a shovel and words of encouragement if she decided to jump in with both feet. I also carried extra clothing for her sympathizers, should they arrive.

The moment she dreaded the most finally arrived. It was time for us to take that long stroll out to the mega-dumpster, where nightmares become a reality by the sheer sight of its imposing volume. The mere presence of this beast is enough to stifle any motivation for a search effort. Surveying the sea of garbage, Becky admitted that everything looked identical. Grimacing, the young excavator hoped to become lucky on the first dig, or perhaps the second. Picking through the trash like Hinckley's buzzards, she barely broke the surface. As she rummaged through a dumpster that was near capacity, Becky gradually relinquished hope, like a despondent fugitive. She was living this bad dream.

After ten minutes of unproductive labor, it was evident we were going nowhere and decided to throw in the towel. Well aware of the preaching she would endure upon returning home from school that day, Becky had to concoct a story believable to her parents. "I forgot it was on my tray," or "It was accidentally left on the table and the janitor threw it away" usually invoked sympathy. It got them off the hook and made me look like the bad guy. There was always a story told, and each version had its own rendition.

This would be a great opportunity for the self-styled entrepreneur to generate the ortho retainer warranty. You know, a little insurance on the side. In my day, we just wrapped the darn thing in napkins and jammed it into our pockets. Any losses accrued would be reimbursed via berry fields. But the times, they are changing. Alas, the burden shifted to the parents to drop a bundle on the orthodontist for the sake of their deduction. Nice break, kiddo.

Time is always inadequate between lunches, with plenty of real estate to cover. Lollygagging is not an option. Call me

Johnnie-come-lately, as I arrive belatedly to trash piling ever higher, tables that need cleaning, and students requiring supervision or babysitting. Once again, my valuable services would be required to retrieve discarded personal items and treasure troves, including family heirlooms. Let us throw in grandma's wedding band for good measure, brought to school by her granddaughter to claim bragging rights. The show-and-tell session given by the middle school blondie suddenly evolved into an attempt to locate. With a search team consisting of classmates, we were fortunate enough to find it, turning tears into cheers.

Immediately, I lectured the student with this piece of advice: "If this wedding band is important to you, you'll probably want to leave it home." It was advice well heeded. This should not come as a surprise, but most students prefer a dumpster-diving partner. With pleas of desperation, they convince an unsuspecting friend to spend a portion of their lunch break dressed in salvage gear. Wearing jumbo neoprene gloves and oversized rain slickers, they are a remarkable sight. Misery loves company, but company doesn't always reciprocate.

Fads and Fashions

Bulging with anxious students, bus #54 roared into the school parking lot driven by a man on a mission. Some passengers endured nearly three quarters of an hour of mood extremes, from those suffering sleep deprivation to the handful who contracted motor-mouth syndrome. While companionship and conversation are important, there are days when silence is golden. I have heard the horror stories from students. Some are slightly graphic, yet I receive the juicy details anyway. One eccentric senior, labeled them "freaks and psychos" that occupied adjacent seats. Perhaps we're trending in the wrong direction. Frankly readers, I have to tell you that some of my experiences on a bus at the wheel could be scenes out of "One Flew Over the Cuckoos Nest." Later in this book you'll understand what I had to deal with. As school bus drivers will tell you, they never promise a rose garden, only a seat and their best intentions of a safe arrival.

A hint of diesel wafted in the parking lot as Lenny applied the air brakes, arriving at the point of debarkation. It was time to condition myself mentally for an influx of chatter and a parade of fashion. The doors burst open, and the staff prepared themselves to receive their daily dose of wardrobe deficiencies.

Parents, do you know what your teenagers are wearing, or in many cases not wearing, to school? It is a logical question, and one that warrants an answer. Contemplate for a moment if you will. Would you not assume their attire, if inadequate, would raise some eyebrows or attract the wrong kind of attention? A brief observation of their revealing apparel should be reason enough to deliver an ultimatum before they leave your property and enter the school grounds. Perhaps you are not home to greet them because you have that early morning commute.

On my average day, I see a cross section of fashions initially as they enter the cafeteria, transforming the campus into a micro tabloid vogue. What happens next may cause periodic neck contortions. The remaining staff view the final cut as students proceed to their first-period class. A culture clash occurs, and it can get downright ugly.

Guys, why do you enjoy wearing those cargo shorts, with the hem inching toward the ankles? I get confused. It places the beltline somewhere around the crotch, and that should be known to cause some discomfort. Sagging fashion jeans finish a close second on my gripe list. In either case, everyone receives a visual of your lustrous Skivvies, whether they like it or not. Personally, I find this fad tasteless and provocative.

Day after day, like a broken record, I had to remind Albert, a student assisting me, that he was losing his pants. Meanwhile, I was losing my patience. Enough already—it was time to deliver an ultimatum of my own. "Find a belt or you're out of a job!" Maybe you are thinking I was a little too strict. Well, after a five-minute observation, I had all the Sponge Bob characters memorized.

Echoing my thoughts were the voices of the administrators in a chorus mode, commanding "pull 'em up." Was that too much to ask, or should the school district have provided suspenders? If something like that wouldn't bring this fad to a screeching halt, it would certainly create an air of nostalgia. Imagine when this kid ventured out into the real world applying for a real job, what would that be like? I pitied his future employer.

While the guys can have their moments, the women on the other hand have a tendency to be more flagrant violators of the dress code. It is no surprise that many teenage girls wish to maintain that pop star image. Here at Evergreen Valley High, we perceive a bit of competition with Hollywood's sex symbols when dealing with the cleavage quandary. Their low-cut fashion tops serve as both an attraction and distraction. Occasionally, they will go overboard and captivate the wrong audience, as a student named Ashley once did. She appeared one morning in the breakfast line with her body autographed in all the wrong places and claimed bragging rights. The kitchen staff blew the whistle, and the administrators began seeking the graphic artist responsible. Upon interrogation, Miss Body Expression received more attention than she anticipated and a one-way ticket home.

I used to shudder every time I saw someone's tongue pierced with a stud and wondered if it altered their sense of taste. I think I have recently adapted to the fad that is becoming all too popular. With various pieces of metal attached to their skin, I still marvel how they pass airport security. There are likely to be bells and whistles going off, delaying everyone's departure. One day I was responding to an incident and accidentally walked through a modeling session being conducted in a hallway. Between the piercings and tattoos, I labeled it a body mutilation convention. Any further description is TMI.

Girls, I have an additional legitimate complaint. Is it possible to be more discreet with your personal items, i.e., feminine hygiene products? Someone has to purge the mess you leave behind, and it will likely be your janitor or custodian.

One day it happened. Our middle school secretary practically begged me to make an appearance outside a girls' restroom. Upon my arrival, laughter greeted me in lieu of embarrassment. I glanced at the ceiling, and then glared at the girls. It was obvious they desired to entertain themselves at the staff's expense by observing our reactions. These vexatious little pranksters displayed a vulgarity that sent shock waves through the halls. Did they succeed in grossing out the vice principal? You can bet the farm on it.

All eyes were on the custodian. It was time to position my ladder and proceed with this tasteless removal procedure. I donned my latex gloves as two female students stood nearby, giggling. Apparently, they were unfazed by the two items I plucked from the ceiling although the teachers were certainly relieved. I digress.

OUR VERSION OF THE BAD BOY

Envision a student who could torment every staff member from administrators to nomadic groundskeepers, while simultaneously portraying himself as the perfect gentleman. Did such a persona exist? He did in my world, and what you end up with is a Jekyll and Hyde personality. Some would say he was trapped in someone else's body. Had he lived in the fifties, he would have fit in with the "Greaser Gang" cult. He looked and lived the part. I have conversed with numerous staff members over the years regarding memories of students, and it is inevitable that the name of a certain deviant character surfaces whenever we reminisce. Just as the theme song from a popular TV drama denotes, our high school featured its own version of the "bad boy." The wrinkles and the gray hairs or premature baldness are indicators of what our staff had to weather during their tenure. In fact, I believe we earned more than our share during the time a student named Eddie attended our high school. Not only did he gain notoriety, he perfected it.

Eddie presented himself as being debonair, a ladies man. A quick observation of the female entourage that customarily tagged along affirmed his star status. His magnetic charm was likely one of the reasons why he was wildly popular with the girls, posing as a modern day Pied Piper.

Eddie was an actor as well, who exercised a dark side. Known for his juvenile-delinquent tactics, he was typical of the Bart Simpson ilk. To draw attention to himself, he constructed a crude metal and plastic addition that resembled a bubble. Then he attached it to the top of his gas guzzling Plymouth Savoy. Modifying his vehicle, giving it that extraterrestrial look, was standard fare for this dude, but we will never know or understand why he demolished his taillights.

One fair-weather morning, Eddie did the unthinkable. He tried to jump over a culvert, ended up in a ditch, and overturned in front of fellow classmates, while attempting to imitate Hollywood stuntmen. It was the debut of his acting career. Not only did Eddie capture the attention of the staff, he evoked sympathy among some of the high school girls. While most of us were in lockup mode from laughter, his female coterie seemed quite concerned and came to his aid like nurses in the ER. Miraculously, he escaped with only minor abrasions and possibly a bruised ego.

Eddie certainly would have qualified as a finalist in the worst-dressed category among celebrities, had he attained that status. Every day was clash day, since nothing in his wardrobe matched. Intentionally, of course. His strange and unconventional apparel included red, white, and blue-striped pants with a brilliant orange shirt to match. Or perhaps it was green plaid slacks paired with a hot-pink long-sleeved shirt and polka dot tie. It didn't matter what he wore. Regardless of the attire he chose for the day, his general appearance resembled a nostalgia battle from the 60s to the 90s.

How did an individual of his caliber become a friend to some and a foe to others? It depended on the incident. That was part of Eddie's current game plan, whatever game he played. He made the first move, his presence becoming known when he scattered unopened milk cartons at various locations throughout the school. It became his trademark in a somewhat twisted way. Copycats surfaced and tried to imitate him, but they failed to command the same attention as Eddie. The cooks were always suspicious when his alter ego came through the lunch line, and sometimes they went ballistic in the aftermath. Occasionally caught off guard, the kitchen staff would find chewing tobacco in selected food dishes. They suspected who was behind these dastardly deeds; yet, they could never prove it. The evidence against him was indisputable, but no one could build a case. All the cooks' hard work was eventually tossed into the trash.

If there was one unanimous idiosyncrasy about this child, it was the element of surprise involving his victims. One day our high school secretary, Mrs. Kinney, called me on the two-way radio to meet Mr. Rigler at a specific location in one of our hallways. What could be so earth shattering that I had to pull myself away from a women's restroom stall? Not just any stall, but one that had assumed the characteristics of a message board. Before texting became popular, some girls would voice their opinions of each other and leave it for me to read. It was tacky but effective. Our principal knew I had a lot of real estate to cover, and altering my plans to meet somewhere meant a post-disaster scenario. Yet, I am thankful he made the discovery, not I.

Maintaining my composure and restraint, I surveyed the situation and noticed a contrast in the body expressions of the two individuals present. On the one hand was Eddie, slouching moderately and revealing one of his counterfeit facial smirks, beneath that disgusting mullet. By contrast, Mr. Rigler (a transplanted Razorback) scowled with a look of repugnance and shook his head in utter disbelief at yet another episode of Eddie's shenanigans. His behavior was inexplicable in any logical terms. He had deliberately spilled soda pop on the floor, covering a sizable area, then offered to clean it. I thought I had heard everything, until he presented his commentary. Eddie wanted to experience a janitor's duties for himself. Mr. Hyde's character had reared its ugly head.

While Mr. Rigler stood guard over the puddle, I prepared a concoction of water and cleaning solution in my mop bucket. Next, I gave the schmuck a demonstration of how to mop the floor properly. I explained the procedure while biting my lip to avoid saying something I might regret later. Infuriated, I gave Eddie the mop and observed him cleaning the floor under the watchful eyes of the principal. He completed the task he so desperately wanted to experience and presumably felt some type of satisfaction. Almost immediately, our frustrated administrator headed back to his office with Eddie in tow.

Who could second-guess what he would do next? His pranks were endless and provoking, putting the staff on notice wherever he graced us with his presence. On the verge of going postal, Mrs. Winn tried to decipher his rambling notes and unexcused absences. Was it an authentic parent signature, or was it his? Who took credit for it? Was he tardy, did he arrive on time, or did he leave and return? These questions were repeatedly asked and debated.

A frail Mrs. Winn was retirement bound, yet she failed to realize Eddie would accelerate the process. He always found a way to manipulate teachers. Lunchtime discussions turned to strategy sessions. Frequently, it became impossible to discern fact from fiction. He was a real character in his private drama world. One thing is certain: the mold was broken when Eddie finally left us, and no one has replaced him to this day.

I returned my mop to the janitor's closet, once a place of safe refuge but now the locale for general pillaging, and thought for a moment; I had been tested long before Eddie arrived on the scene. I reminisced about the elementary school students who enjoyed a janitor's debut as much as the appearance of Viola Swamp, the nefarious substitute for Miss Nelson. Turf invasions bring about questions. "What is he doing here?" for instance. After a couple weeks of intense scrutiny, the children embraced me as a settler instead of an invader.

My perception of grade school innocence almost transformed, due to one sole child. In my eyes, I visualized most elementary students as the next generation, usually amiable but needing guidance. Then one day reality struck and my eyes were opened.

The principal approached me and asked if I was interested in some extra cash. All I had to do was study to become a bus driver. I failed to grasp at the time what I was getting into. Affirming my intentions, I began intensive weekend training, utilizing the bus driving for dummies handbook. Not exactly a cakewalk. I offered to shuttle your child from home to school and back for a stipend, and I enjoyed each unique personality. However, there were moments when I met defiance and days when I deserved hazard pay. To all those tried and true bus drivers, I think we are on the same page.

There is always at least one rebellious child that requires extra attention while you do everything in your power to maintain control of the bus. Language becomes an issue when dealing with a child who is the equivalent of the evil Chucky. Whatever Brad spoke in my presence would have embarrassed those egregious gangster rappers. Some of the tales he told of events or activities at home were raucous and explicit in nature. I empathized with any babysitter that survived one evening with him. I pitied the students tormented by his drivel, since most sought to be reclusive. While we longed for peace and quiet, he babbled incessantly.

There were minimal alternatives for consequences, and duct tape was not an option. This one child gave me more migraines than all other students combined, a monumental achievement for a second grader. Some days I wondered what he had eaten for breakfast, or if he had eaten breakfast at all. Deficient or excessive meds played a pivotal role in his erratic behavior. I kept a supply of sugar packets for the days he curled up in his seat, listless and almost incoherent, and I felt like an administering physician. If there was only a way to share his meds, both of us would be on the same plane.

Occasionally, Brad would jump from seat to seat, bus in motion, just to attract my attention. He succeeded. Some students marveled at this child's circus stunts and applauded, but I saw otherwise. The best and safest method to bring this kid back to earth again was to pull the bus to the side of the road. I would dish out a lecture reminiscent of those old-time fiery preachers that was designed specifically for him, but with a captivated audience. It was the equivalent of talking to myself.

Everyone became subjected to this charade at least once a week. Wanting to remain the center of attention, Brad taunted the students almost daily.

In a discussion one day with the principal, I discovered I could gain the upper hand. With the stroke of a pen, I could make him disappear. I had the power and authority to issue a citation, a marvelous invention. That was his ticket off the bus and my ticket to freedom from him for three days. It was celebration time!

Then there was a day when a student threatened me with bodily harm, sending me into shock mode. I would not allow one bump in the road to alter my lifestyle and continued driving. I guess some moments of fortitude can reward you. The reluctant parents met with the principal, their son was suspended, and a written apology was hand delivered to me. So despite the incidents, bus driving has its rewards. Be forewarned, however, whatever grief you cause a bus driver will return to haunt you tenfold.

Please excuse me readers, for a moment, I went off on a tangent, reminiscing about the simplicity of elementary life. I'm sure everyone likes to daydream. I have a tendency to get ahead of myself sometimes; you know how it is. Back to the story at hand.

Like a repeat offender, Eddie received yet another reprimand from our stoic principal, who likely was a candidate for a coronary. Whatever we spoke went in one of Eddie's ears and out the other, with a void in between. The staff proclaimed it selective hearing. In conclusion: students of his caliber are here to boost antacid sales.

Upon returning from the janitor's closet, I began focusing on the upcoming lunch and expected aftermath. At least I had avoided one situation that day, no calls for body fluids. Any day without that (cleanup) is a good day. Tranquility is always welcomed in my world; however, that was not to be. Custodians do not enjoy such luxuries. The atmosphere was about to change with an anxious voice transmitting over my two-way radio. Like a slap in the face, it brought me back to reality. All hell was about to break loose.

OPERATION: CODE BROWN

I dread one type of cleanup, particularly when it occurs before or during lunch. Let's say 75 percent of the time it amounts to nothing. Yet, it is the other 25 percent that can place teachers in lockdown and, for some students, cause a visual chain reaction. You know, the kid that shouldn't have shown up at school but Mom says, "You are going anyway." In cases like this, I suggest we send Jimmy home with a wastebasket as a gentle reminder, and so we have. The morning had already sucked from dealing with Brad, so I could not imagine the volcano blowing its top. However, as expected, the urgent call arrived via our high school secretary's dysfunctional radio, proclaiming the imminent cataclysm.

Mrs. Kinney's voice quavered, "Fifty-two, Fifty-two do you copy?" Unfortunately, fifty-two is my number, and anyone listening on that frequency would be tuned-in to Suspense Network Radio, including bus drivers. We had to keep the conversations prudent and inoffensive to meet broadcast guidelines. A gentle slip of the tongue could get you called on the carpet. The punctuation in her delivery meant breaking news was about to be reported. With apprehension, I responded to a once-serene employee that appeared flustered and confused, like the TV anchorwoman losing her video feed. "All the toilets in the agricultural building have backed up and overflowed into neighboring classrooms! Can you please check that out?" I had encountered the standard problem with one or maybe two commodes. How would I deal with ten? Armed with lighting equipment and dueling plungers in each hand, I prepared to engage in battle.

A myriad of thoughts dashed through my mind as I approached the building, yet somehow I had to remain optimistic. Radio calls have a history of becoming blown out of proportion because the reporter (usually a student) who notifies the secretary has a tendency to exaggerate to the Nth degree. Being naturally skeptical, I approached the building, anticipating a fifteen—to twenty-minute mucking out. I opened the door and realized Mrs. Kinney had made no mistake. It was a clip right out of a sci-fi movie, perhaps *The Creeping Crud*. Athletic shoes and sneakers were never designed for this type of disaster.

In adjacent classrooms, students began jockeying desks as seeping sewage made its ghastly, unwelcome appearance. The unmistakable odor that followed began wafting into that section of the old metal building. Neither fire nor flood could decommission this aging monstrosity. If anything did occur to alter a teacher's day of instruction, a comment had once been made that it would take a wrecking ball to bring this building down.

The first casualty would become Miss Smothers's Spanish class. It always endured the brunt of the spillovers and changed her program lineup. Cinco de Mayo became Stinko de Mayo. I ditched the plungers in the janitors' closet where I searched for a bailing bucket. Nada. Zilch. A laughable idea I admit, but desperate people do desperate things. Located directly behind the restrooms were a storage room and a darkroom for developing photos. The gateway to both rooms was mechanical drawing class. I had no choice but to watch the disaster unfold before my eyes. First, it was imperative I muster up some courage. Then I needed a strategy and plan for the massive cleanup. Abdicating was not an option.

Encroaching upon the hallway, this malodorous mixture began mapping out its own course. That left me with no alternative but to don rubber boots, grab a flashlight, and prepare to charge into the art room. Some students became frantic watching the sludge seep in and sought higher ground, as if watching the return of the blob. I opened the classroom door to the art room, and my worst fears materialized. That creeping crud had backed up into the room's sinks, creating an unbearable working environment. It appeared we had reached the point of no return. Those beautiful drawings were abandoned, and the students had no choice except to flee like roaches at sunup.

Screams were heard in the distance, as students in the dark room suddenly realized what was invading their space. As I maneuvered my way through a revolving door, my first reaction was to turn on the light. I needed some visual clarity of this manmade cataclysm that was now surrounding me. Flashlight in hand, I peered in, focusing on eyes in the dark that resembled deer in headlights. Enter the brave custodian and exit Amanda, the girl wearing flip-flops. In a panic, students began sloshing out of the darkroom as the depth reached nearly three inches. Forget the bucket, we were approaching level-three flood declaration. A super vacuum from a local porta potty company was the only one-way ticket out of this cesspool. As I reached for the light switch, I discovered photograph negatives hanging from a wire line over a table. All that hard work and effort, jeopardized with the flip of a switch. Feeling empathy for our potential future photographers, I kept the flashlight on while I assessed the damage created by that hideous slime. Minus the flames, the place looked like hell, and if it already looked like hell, how could anyone improve the appearance?

As I began to garner all the cleaning supplies that existed, the help I anticipated finally arrived to bail me out, literally. Deliverance came in the form of Rescue Rooter, if only for a moment. Teachers were relieved, and students began cheering for the man who they assumed could rescue them. Never assume anything folks, never.

In this case, Murphy's Law went into effect, and there was one more final twist to this bizarre episode. The plumber dude sent a mini-cam down the septic line to investigate. There are cams for every job, but this had to be the filthiest. The discovery yielded a collapsed line four feet below the surface. This meant tearing up the parking lot with a backhoe, replacing the pipe, and removing every obstruction that had been flushed down. Both restrooms were boarded up for a couple days, while portable toilets became the norm. This brought mixed reactions from everyone. For the staff, it was like the good ole days your grandparents used to recollect. Some opportunistic students decided it would be a nice location for a tryst.

Three grueling hours, two cans of air freshener, and one gallon of disinfectant later, all affected classrooms became habitable once again. Even the restrooms were restored to their pristine condition, which usually only occurs prior to the opening day of school. On this day, records were broken for the longest and most extensive floor makeover of all time, to be remembered for years to come. Every drop of waste was collected and properly disposed of, placing me on a par with hazmat. Visions of a hot shower danced in my brain.

The moment had arrived for damage control, and, unfortunately, many items in the classrooms were partially submerged. Some became floating islands for any fleeing rodents seeking asylum in the nearby tilled fields. Our distressed art teacher, Mrs. Landau, opted for a salvage operation and recovered what came to a paltry amount. Textbooks and art supplies generally do not fare well when exposed to liquid elements. Brushing her dark shoulder-length hair back, our fair-skinned educator tried to remain positive to the end. Suffering the greatest loss of any staff member in the building, the disaster declaration had taken its toll. Mrs. Landau requested two trashcans and a stockpile of cleaning supplies. Words of wisdom: should you leave anything on the floor in the proximity of a restroom, its final destination may be the trash bin.

As I was applying the last touches to the girls' loo, the dismissal bell rang. Some classrooms on the northeast side of the building miraculously escaped the deluge, and students emptied out into the hallway. The job skills and automotive classes originated from that direction, and many were clueless of the nature of the calamity. Catching the eye of at least one staff member—who had a comment for everything—his ambiguous statement created a moment of mirth in the midst of real-time school drama: "S—t happens."

How can you argue with that?

LOCKER MOMENTS TO REMEMBER

"We have a student locked inside a locker with the door jammed, and the key won't open it." A simple prank suddenly became a desperate moment for both the student and his would-be rescuers. Where was the locksmith when you needed him? When I received this bizarre radio call, it made me wonder what was going through the incarcerated student's mind.

Not a day goes by that our secretary, totally immersed in her desktop, isn't called upon to open a jammed locker—with limited success. The moment inevitably emerges when I am suddenly atop the secretary's most-wanted list, and for a good reason.

The purpose of a locker is two-fold. Accommodate as many personal items as one can cram inside, and continue to provide job security for the custodian. Several staff members have suggested the school simply eliminate them. I can just visualize the hallways lined with backpacks, cosmetic stations, trinkets, and ineffable objects unbefitting the puritan's eye. Refugee camps, I tell you.

On any given day, simply walk down the halls and survey the mélange of students' paraphernalia projecting out of the locker doors. The ultimate challenges continue to be the backpack strap or wayward shoelace wrapped around the locking mechanism. Unlatching the door could translate into opening a Pandora's Box. Once inside, I may recover a cache of half-eaten lunches emitting who knows what kind of fermented odor.

Thrust into the spotlight one day was this particular student, who had drawn attention to himself as the result of a dare. Predictably, this occurred at the behest of his friend, who was more of a hindrance than a help. As a middle school student, thoughts of being caught do not cross your mind, only the ambition to squeeze into a locker to impress your friends. This ritual has occurred since the birth of these metal contraptions, and every episode is . . . unique. Failure to escape is a probability.

When my radio began broadcasting a distress call from a high-strung secretary concerning this over-inquisitive student—who's curiosity had led to his eventual imprisonment—she cried, "He may have trouble breathing; your presence is needed now! Do you have a copy fifty-two?" Perhaps this call had 911 written all over it, but I had to render that decision upon my arrival. As the rescuer, I would determine whether it was a real life and death matter.

I arrived with a hammer and pry bars to a scene so bizarre it drew spectators from all directions. The locker was latched at the top, with a pair of feet protruding from the bottom motionlessly. Talk about solitary confinement; this middle school child was immediately becoming aware of the inconceivable predicament in which he had placed himself. I wasted no time, and the door popped open in a heartbeat amid cheers and the occasional question. "Cody, can you breathe?" Perspiring and nearly stricken with terror, the young daredevil emerged unscathed and tried to regain his composure before a live audience. Among those in attendance waiting to greet him were various dignitaries, including the vice principal. Dread, doom, and detention awaited him, and that was only the beginning. Our Houdini had wanted to realize his dream of fitting inside a locker while his friend conveniently shut the door. Oh, one slight detail; the door did not close completely. So plan in advance if entertaining viewers.

An interesting scenario developed once this student was extricated. At roughly 5'6" and 120 pounds, this dark-haired, wide-eyed prankster enjoyed plenty of head space, but minimal body room. I noticed the door now included an impression that was strikingly similar to the contour of his body, prompting a spontaneous mini-conference with the administrators. The Powers That Be determined there was only one reasonable financial solution—I had no choice but to replace the locker door at the expense of the student and his family. It was time for this joker to despoil his piggybank and cough up some cold, hard cash. I could not think of a better way to make an impression than to punish him right where it hurts—in the wallet.

As wacky as that incident turned out, another case of "I can definitely fit inside" created additional controversy. A conversation heard by anyone listening on our radio frequency was right out of the *Rescue 911* archives. The junior-high secretary, Mrs. McKinley (nicknamed Agent 99), requested a cutting torch and my expertise at breaking and entering. This pained me considerably because anyone that knows me knows that my experience with a cutting torch sucks. Just give me a pair of bolt cutters and I can do some damage. So once again, with visions of an immediate release, and pry bars and hammer in hand, I arrived at the scene of the incident.

I had never failed to break into a locker, and that day was not going to be the day. I arrived to a cluster of rubbernecking students and their incessant questioning. "Kelsey, are you okay?" "What's it like inside?" No response . . . labored breathing. I inserted my key, and then pounded on the door handle with a hammer and screwdriver. This released pressure on the door, allowing it to pop open instantly. It also created that disturbing metal on metal sound, drawing the occasional teacher out of their class to announce, "Oh, it's you!" Middle school girls became weirded-out upon watching the spectacle. Everyone noticed that Kelsey was in a state of near hyperventilation. Due to her small stature, she'd wedged herself inside the locker almost perfectly, like a circus contortionist. What may seem like an innocent stunt to attract attention could ultimately have become a precarious situation. Some students are known to thrive on danger.

With your curiosity aroused, you may be asking, "What is the worse thing you've ever found in a locker?" I've discovered crude and tasteless items over the years, and some of them could very well be photographs. I will leave that to your wild and uninhibited imagination. At least two vulgar practical jokes were played in which all the victims were females, and both cases were repulsively similar.

As you probably guessed, I received the call and performed the dirty work. Someone had to do it.

I have to admit being skeptical when two aspiring high school girls requested I bring some cleaning supplies to their glamour catchall. Something was going down, and I was the one stuck in the middle of it. They said the smell was nasty and refused to divulge the contents. They had the perfect excuse. Without further delay, I arrived with the body-fluid cleanup kit and all the accessories contained therein to a locker emitting a distinct odor. Those inquisitive gawkers began arriving for the show. I inserted my key, pulled up on the handle, and cautiously opened the door from behind. Plastered on the inside was a foamy substance that looked and smelled like human waste. Do you think some students have too much time on their hands? Since the content was foam, the cleanup was easy, but the smell permeated the locker. In cases such as these, it would only seem fitting to use air freshener with a baby powder scent to neutralize the odor and spice things up. The girls eventually confessed they knew who did it, yet never reported them. Instead, they had a good laugh at my expense, while I performed the cleanup. It didn't seem quite fair, but then again, nothing in life is fair. As a co-worker once stated, "It all pays the same."

How is it possible to eclipse the previous practical joke? With a little forethought, one can always attempt to outdo those bizarre un-pleasantries. Seniors are particularly adept at this. In this instance, the stories of the two victims were enough to summon our principal away from his office. It had to be earthshattering and sometimes tears help the cause. Mr. Rigler and I gathered at the locker of the two female athletes who had requested our presence. I immediately had suspicions that repair work would become cleanup instead. Someone was out to make life hell for these two students and ruin their day. All eyes were on the locker as I cautiously opened the door. Immediately, one of the girls burst into tears. "How could someone do this to me?" she sobbed. Our principal frowned at the sight, while I thought of the best method of retrieval. It was lame. It was also cruel and unusual punishment. Someone went through a lot of trouble to bring in doggie doo and place it in a towel on the top shelf. While it made for an easy disposal, it did not diminish the impact it had on one of the two girls, still reeling from the shock.

Perhaps there was a clash of personalities among friends? Or, maybe it was a disgruntled former boyfriend with a grudge? However you look at it, I'm sure you're curious as to who the prankster was.

The principal conducted his own CSI to determine what kind of enemies these volleyball players could possibly have had. We can only thank the notable inventor of the video camera to answer that question. As everyone knows, cameras do not lie. With the process of elimination, it didn't take long to narrow the suspect list and ID the perpetrator. The principal gathered both parties together and, to the utter disbelief of the athletes, it was one of their own teammates.

A Recipe for Disaster

What could a school cook possibly do that would create chaos in the facility's kitchen? The answer to that question can be summarized in three words: accidents will happen. It is inevitable! Hungry students reach for their favorite entrée as the cooks try to jockey into position to refill a rapidly disappearing side dish. Folks, it's a zoo. Judging from the way some students act in the lunch line, you have to wonder: is that where a percentage received their upbringing? The cooks are bombarded incessantly, and there are occasions when they simply struggle to stay ahead. These kitchen ladies are an unappreciated lot, frequently going unnoticed for the labor they perform daily. Slaving over a blazing stove and endlessly prepping the food for those ravenous appetites, they are constantly in a time crunch. We only need to wear their apron for an hour—as I have done—to get an idea of how their engaged operation functions.

Yes, yours truly raised a few eyebrows and drew a few cheers when I donned a smock and shuttled pizzas to the serving line. On another occasion, I transported some meaty chicken nuggets that were likely subjected to plumping. Bottom line: when the kitchen is down two cooks and the sub is a no-show, they need all the help they can get. They are desperate; they will take anyone that's ambulatory. Do make the best effort not to get in the way, as there have been some near collisions. Since no one is perfect, however, there was that one day when something unexpected happened, with definite comical overtones.

So I get this call from the secretary asking, no, *urging* me to make an appearance in the kitchen ASAP.

What are these ladies up to now? I wondered. Did one of the cooks unintentionally leave an appendage sample in the garbage disposal? That rare incident merited her the nickname "stubby;" but even more, it showed us how fragile the human body really is. Perhaps it was the day the dishwasher decided to self-destruct and spew water all over the dish room floor, to the amazement of the kitchen help. The worst-case-scenario I could envision was opportunistic students fully engaged in some malfeasance to gain notoriety in the absence of administrators. Like an end to a drought, you can smell the rain coming.

Fearing some minor calamity had transpired, I entered the kitchen breathless, exhausted after sprinting like wounded game, which has a tendency to make heads turn. Running is usually not an option unless the fire alarm is blaring. You know, the district really should consider a shuttle service or providing a scooter for me. The sounds of the 60s and 70s were blaring on the radio. These ladies do enjoy their oldies, and as long as it doesn't interfere with their work, I'm all for it. Thankfully, there was no water leak, no medical emergency, and no food fight. Instead, I tried desperately to hold back the laughter as I observed some of our cooks frantically trying to scoop up a mountain of spilled gravy. The bubbling hot entrée had never arrived at its intended destination, just missing the serving line by the length of a cookie sheet. If I could have picked the right song for the moment, the classic "Clean up Woman" would have fit the bill.

Realizing their plight, I created a makeshift dam utilizing a hamper full of kitchen towels. This caused the gravy to ooze between the floor mats. It may not have spurred much laughter in the heat of the moment, but it would be the topic of discussion for days to come. The rush of students filing through the lunch lines simply added to a chaotic situation. The aroma of sizzling turkey gravy—permeated the area, the substance creating a slick coating on the floor. Four serving lanes were reduced to three to avoid accidents and surfer wannabees. All we needed now was a National Safety Health and Accident Rep. to appear. Wet-floor signs were added as a precaution and to keep liabilities down. Yes, there is always the opportunist who would like nothing more than a free ride in life. Another student tried to muscle his way through the roadblock claiming to be next in line and was threatened with a referral.

Glancing at the kitchen floor, I realized it was a losing battle, and it became evident I didn't have a prayer with a wetmop. I may as well have used a ladle, so I left momentarily and returned with a scoop shovel. While Bettie (one of our cooks) held the shovel, I pushed a floor squeegee, and with a little teamwork, we quickly contained the potato topping. I made a comment that the cleanup bore some resemblance to a barnyard procedure, but instead it was occurring on the kitchen floor. Another cook, Luella, who loved to poke fun at everyone, laughed at the comparison. Bettie remained pensive and refused to yield a smile.

If you have to experience an accident before a live audience, plan for some feedback, if not unexpected fanfare. Also, one must entertain the possibility of an administrator breathing down your neck. As fate would have it, Mr. Rigler arrived in a jovial mood while we demonstrated the gravy removal technique, which was unorthodox to say the least. For small talk, I commented we had just finished a cleanup on aisle one, but you should have been here last week. A grease spill sent me on my duff. The cook responsible for the gravy spill became the victim of a few one-liners, played out to the Late Show's "Top Ten List" for why the incident happened. Apparently feeling remorse, she had apologized, though there was no need for an apology. "These things happen," I told her as I continued mopping the kitchen floor. We were quite the sideshow that day, and America's Funniest Videos audience would have been proud of us.

It Took a Village for This Cleanup

Years ago, our high school campus presented a production that required no rehearsal, and there was no script. However, had one been written, it would have been the antithesis of a *Love Story*. Most likely it would have contained the pomp and vigor of *Rocky*. This screenplay was the perfect paradigm of a tumultuous relationship. Nothing was artificial; it was live and surreal. Do you think there is a secondary school today that is immune to drama, whether it is simulated or authentic? Not likely; it still occurs in bite size portions. Perhaps I should emphasize, we are not *Friday Night Lights*, that prime-time high school soap opera, nor would we want to be. Having said that, and despite the general tranquility this country school enjoys, we have had our share of dramatic incidents. The following presentation was unforgettable and emblazoned in the minds of the participants.

In the eyes of the casual observer, Jake and Alison were the epitome of the perfect duo, like spouses on a TV sitcom. Forget the fact that Jake's body volume was proportionate to a steer bull with an attitude to match. And Alison's tiny frame was dwarfed by her boyfriend. Still, they became quite the campus tabloid couple.

Close friends they associated with, however, painted a disturbing picture through a progression of time. Though the pair had been dating (and I use that word loosely) each other for several months, it became evident the theme song for these two was "Love Rollercoaster." A last-ditch effort to patch things up had failed, and it appeared the relationship was going south. Alison, though generally reserved, could show her true colors when threatened. She could be a firecracker ready to go off. Perhaps a hint of jealousy had crept into the picture. Whatever dispute had occurred between the two would gradually affect those closely associated with the couple. Based on my personal observations, when domestic disputes materialize, they seem to coincide with a full moon. Our lovebirds remained inseparable, and on some occasions it became necessary to pry them apart in order that they would arrive to class on time. That fateful day became the exception. Little did we realize that, as time ticked by, much of our staff would be unwittingly drawn into their relationship. Like a death knell, the classic lovers' spat was performed before an ill-prepared live audience.

It was a day comparable to any other spring day; love was in the air and couples were becoming restless. Some students were anxious to be outside, while others would manipulate a teacher to avoid class. Jake preferred both.

This brawny, blonde-headed linebacker tried to prove a point to Alison and failed in his effort. A shouting match erupted that became as volatile as mixing ammonia and bleach. Jake grew livid, displaying a look of violence that indicated he couldn't hold back any longer. According to those who witnessed the event, their verbal confrontation was the spark that lit the fuse.

When the call for my assistance arrived, there was a real sense of urgency. Immediately, I knew I would need an emergency backup crew. Copious volumes of blood were splattered in a seemingly endless trail. The droplets commenced at an exit door near the cafeteria, progressed down the hallway, and made a sharp left turn down a second hallway. This eerie pathway continued through the entire weight and fitness room, out the double doors, down the main hallway, and finally terminated abruptly at the high school office. Custodians, maintenance, and all available teachers were pressed into action to assist in this extensive cleanup. On second thought, let's forget the concept of cleanup and tell it like it was. I mobilized an emergency triage to save one lone casualty. There were simply not enough wet floor signs to cover the distance, so disinfecting the school was a reasonable description for this ordeal.

In area measurement, it was roughly 100 yards; in loss of blood measurement, Jake could have been a donor for two.

In a fit of rage after an argument with Alison, our hotheaded football athlete turned boxer, took out his frustrations on an exit door window. I need to emphasize, this wasn't your typical, run-of-the-mill plate glass window. Sandwiched between two pieces of glass was an impervious wire mesh that provided added security and portrayed that institutional look. It did what it was designed to do, stop anything dead in its tracks. As Jake's fist penetrated the window, the force caused shards of glass to explode outward, pelting the world at large. When his forearm finally encountered the sharp wires, veins punctured indiscriminately, which caused him to bleed like a stuck hog.

Flipping out due to the life-threatening situation he had put himself in, the last thing on Jake's mind was the path he was going to take to seek immediate medical assistance. Jaws dropped as Jake staggered into the office like a wounded fugitive on the run. Secretaries were converted into nurses and administrators into nurse's aides that day. By the time first aid was applied, one could hardly differentiate between his forearm and a package of hamburger. The bottom of the hourglass was filling rapidly.

The nearest small-town fire department, located almost within an earshot of our campus, responded to the 911 call. Paramedics arrived in a New York minute as the boyfriend slipped into a state of shock. A visibly upset Alison displayed signs of a mental breakdown and was sedated while anxious office personnel observed. Our couple met for the last time before Jake was shuttled away in the meat wagon. "The Love I Lost" appeared to be their departing song.

Like bloodhounds, curious students followed the endless trail, which led them directly to me. An impromptu question-and-answer session was generated as they maneuvered around the volunteers. A few choice comments were uttered, some intelligent, some not. "Whoa dude, someone sure lost a lot of blood! Is he still alive?" "Watch where you're walking you dumb ass, you're stepping in it." And of course, let us not forget the standard, "I like your green gloves." It was evident these young adults had never experienced a trauma scene, as they haphazardly walked through a maze of life fluid and disinfectant.

This ominous state of affairs, resembling the 4077th of *M*A*S*H* fame, underwent a complete metamorphosis. Overall, I was impressed at how the staff handled the crisis and all the positive feedback. Unfortunately, no Oscars were awarded that day, although we could have merited a nomination for best daytime soap opera in a graphic setting. Meanwhile, our bleeder was cruising Code 3 to the emergency room. Contained within a thirty-two-gallon bag were a gazillion used body fluid kits. Everyone watched and wondered: would Jake make it through the night?

Returning to the crime scene, I determined there was a snowball's chance in hell of removing the glass safely. Large dagger-like pieces hung precariously in the middle of the window, resembling a two-edged sword. Gazing in awe at the gaping hole, students uttered words of disbelief that it was a miracle no body parts had been severed. Thanks to the invention of duct tape, which I used to cover the window with a few pieces of plywood, all was safe and secure, hindering any potential mimics (should they materialize) until the glass repairman's arrival the following day. That man definitely earned some serious *dinero*, picking through the rubble and declaring, "It's one of the worst I've seen."

Day two brought more breaking news. As the soap opera continued to advance toward the final curtain, the staff was informed that Jake had survived the ordeal. Statements of gratitude were bestowed upon those who applied the life-saving tourniquet, with one exception. Alison suggested Nurse Ratchet should have administered an additional bandage over Jake's mouth. Some of the finest surgeons at a regional hospital pieced him back together with yards of nylon or polypropylene.

Several days passed, and Jake regained full use of his arm. Ironically, it was the relationship that was finally severed. Had anger management been implemented, there is little doubt the situation would have been different. As tragic love stories go, one violent moment sealed their fate forever.

THOSE OFF-THE-WALL
SCIENCE DELIVERIES

During my senior year in high school, the local fire department had made a few unscheduled visits to the notorious science/chemistry class before the building finally went up in smoke. How many high school students can make that claim? Predictably volatile, those Bunsen burners provide not only a continuous source of education, but also free entertainment. And when improperly attended, these bad boys create excitement unparalleled. Despite the fact that science class had been my least favorite, Mr. Dickerson had a way of creating merriment in an otherwise tedious subject. Thanks to his bubbly personality, he had managed to capture my attention long enough for me to stay focused and endure a class I was so not into. He was the science guru for my era.

While every staff person has specific needs, those inquisitive science teachers (you gotta love 'em) have an insatiable appetite for just-plain-grotesque items. In an effort to keep the students' creative juices flowing, they purchase some of the most hideous educational paraphernalia online via "The Sinister Science Shop" website. And when it arrives, the cardboard box conceals what will develop into their next science experiment, and yours truly receives a first-hand glimpse of what is in store for the unsuspecting students when the surprise package is delivered to the classroom.

On one occasion, a box arrived that aroused my suspicion that it had somehow been wedged under the rear axle of the delivery truck. Methodically, I stacked all the packages on my hand truck and made sure the mangled one was delivered first, for the most obvious reason. As a rule, damaged freight never leaves the receiving office. This unusual parcel was the exception. It didn't look right, it didn't feel right, it didn't smell right. Despite all the negatives, the science lab had a project to accomplish that day and nothing was going to hold Mr. Kimball back. The experiment faced intense, under-the-knife scrutiny of one anxious biology teacher.

I'd been leery about the contents of this delivery for a specific reason. Suddenly and without warning, the package had begun oozing an indistinguishable fluid. Drops of the clear liquid left a noticeable trail, equivalent to a drippy trash bag that isn't monitored. Fortunately, the hallway was foot-traffic free for the moment. My ESP, however, indicated that company was coming—unwanted company.

Unusual incidents have a way of attracting students like magnets attract steel. Remember, it's their innate nature to be curious.

As I made a right turn and progressed down the hallway, a mild yet noxious odor began emanating from the package, bearing a striking resemblance to that foul-smelling black and white mammal we are all familiar with. It was an accident waiting to happen. This unsavory combination brought rubberneckers out of the woodwork, as the parcel appeared to be disintegrating before my eyes. Looking behind me, I realized I had left a trail down the previous hall that prompted the need for wet floor signs. I had previously chosen to leave the hot-pink collection locked away. Apparently, they are a collector's item and periodically end up inside someone's locker. Surely, the students would notice the droplets on the floor and avoid them like body fluids. Dream on. Formaldehyde tracked across the entire hallway, and once again, if anything could go wrong, it did.

Students stormed the science room on my heels like ants at a picnic. By this time, the package had leaked like a ruptured radiator hose, drenching the one beneath it. Portraying the Grim Reaper, I delivered the news. There is no need to schedule any science experiments today Mr. Kimball. One involving your package was already conducted and it tanked. Meticulously, our science/biology teacher opened the remains, while a few students in attendance held that Fear Factor facial expression. With gag reflexes in check, the mystery of the contents was finally revealed: cats, their nine lives having been spent. Who would have thought . . . this should raise the ire of cat lovers everywhere. It never occurred to me that I would be delivering embalmed felines. When shipped, they were nice and neatly packaged in that mysterious, pungent gas, well preserved. If I delayed mopping the floor tile, would it meet a similar fate?

It would be nothing short of a miracle to return this package in the condition it was in when it had been shipped. If there was a positive side to this story, at least I was not required to repack the box. Mr. Kimball would become mentally challenged demonstrating his pack and ship skills. I couldn't wait to see the results. There was no escaping the cleanup, which amounted to a minimal amount of mop strokes and my floor cleaner featuring the bald guy with the earring. Not to mention that the atmosphere improved dramatically once the stink dissipated. One has to wonder why laboratories can't design a gas to smell like perfume. Look what the gas company did with natural gas, and they created the odor for safety reasons. Thanks to the advancement of science, formaldehyde is now available sans the stench. I think it would be more janitor-friendly if that pungent gas odor resembled chocolate chip cookies instead.

As spoiled deliveries go, they are rare, costly in large quantities, and a great topic for discussion. On another occasion, a package destined for the science lab began exuding that all-too-familiar odor again. This time, however, the secretary and I mutually agreed that no movement was in our best interest. We convinced the teacher he needed to personally inspect the contents and assess the damage. Emulating a "don't worry, be happy" attitude, he refused to let this incident ruin his day. Fumbling with the wrappings, he finally uncovered his prized possessions: one poorly packaged container of piglet fetuses. Due to the mediocre condition in which they were discovered, they never went under the knife. Or, a better yet unpleasant way to put it was, decomposition was in progress. Alternately, the little piggies were re-housed in a plastic bag to avoid any premature departure via the dumpster. Once again, Mr. Kimball demonstrated his unorthodox wrapping skills.

The pressure was now on our office secretary, Shelly, to contact the trucking company that delivered the miniscule porkers. Our generally persuasive secretary jumped on the landline and pleaded her case. Like fighting city hall, Shelly's request was ignored. The earliest pickup time was twenty-four-hours later and not a moment sooner. As you can imagine, our secretary was beside herself. She was stuck babysitting the tiny hams for the rest of the day. Little did she realize when she'd been hired that this would become part of her job description. A word to the wise: read the fine print before filling out that application.

Thankfully, the remaining deliveries were completed that day, but I had to pick up some loose ends. I was given the unpleasant task of explaining to some faculty members why their packages appeared somewhat deflated and smelled like death. Most did not seem care, provided their parcel arrived in one piece. Since the holidays were approaching, some female staff members were wishing they had something for their sweet tooth. Where are those boxes of chocolates when you need one?

Flaming Hot Wheels

Being an inquisitive child and engaging in a moment of roguishness growing up may have played a decisive factor in my adult life when it comes to safety. An incident I will never forget concerns the time I found a book of matches in the basement of our two-story rental. Thankfully, I realized their destructive power before the house went up in flames, thus terminating my brief reign as arsonist. The hide tanning I received was warranted, and being humiliated in the presence of my matriarchal grandmother because of that malicious act spoke for itself.

Fire, it consumes your attention, as it consumes what lies in its path. Emotions become elevated regardless of whether you are directly accountable for creating this scenario or simply a bystander. Your inability to quell the flames is your worst nightmare. If you are employed in a school district, this unpredictable event is guaranteed to provide an adrenaline rush, while also testing your response time. It breeds excitement among the student body, sending them to text message heaven. Once the fire alarm activates, the unknown can be daunting. Having been a Cub Scout, being prepared is my motto. And for you thrill seekers remember, life comes at you fast.

What transpired one early winter's day after Y2K could have occurred at any particular school on any random day. Unfortunately, it was ours.

It was a damp December afternoon when an assemblage of students strolled across the parking lot to the high school agricultural building. This post-60s monstrosity aka the building ready for demolition, holds a variety of elective classes in hopes of producing the next high-rise architect or the top exporter of wool. The choices are diverse; so, whatever floats your boat.

The color of the restroom walls was always a topic for discussion. I often received requests to transform the nearly flamingo-pink girls bathroom into anything *but* pink. "When can you paint our restroom blue, just like the boys' restroom?" sighed a couple of senior girls on a mission. Eventually, I would honor their request, though they had to settle for institutional white. You would have thought I was painting a portrait, based on the *oohs* and *aahs*.

Like weary travelers stuffing airline luggage, student backpacks were maxed out from storing books, athletic gear, and occasional items prohibited by law, i.e., chewing tobacco. Let us not forget those numerous students who partake in after-school activities and whose primary source of transportation is the school bus. Little did this collective group realize, they were about to exit their comfort zone and enter into a world of chaos.

Inside the auto shop, one area was heating up like a Texas cookout as students Taylor and Breanna began performing some minor maintenance on their 1966 Ford Mustang Coupe. It was a classic. Taylor had racing in his blood, while Breanna was a cowgirl at heart. Mr. Swanson, the auto shop teacher, wasted no time lecturing them on the precautions they must take while using their welding rods.

A former drill sergeant, he would breathe down their necks to make his point. It was fourth period, early afternoon, and our metals instructor needed two reliable students. There was no time for a dog and pony show, it was business as usual. Would those repairs be finished in time for the holidays? Best friends, Taylor and Ryan, were counting on it. Ryan performed his share second period, so the pressure fell on Taylor to avoid keeping those ladies waiting. Attached to the Mustang was a flatbed trailer, ready to be used as a float in the upcoming Christmas Parade. Taylor and Ryan's girlfriends were on tap to appear on that float. The time to get their souped-up wheels back on the asphalt was closing in. It was do or die.

Repairs were on schedule, and the boys were on track toward reaching their goals when the fuel line ignited like a backyard barbecue flare-up. There are always risks involved. While it is not impossible for this to occur when these types of repairs are performed, one never expects it. As the events began to unfold, Breanna accidentally burned a hole in the fuel line and ignited vapors in the gas tank. Sparks from the gas line ignited decorations that were left on the trailer. It was virtually a lost cause at that point, creating a volatile scenario. This comes with a warning; under ideal conditions anyone could become a human torch.

Taylor grabbed his Mountain Dew that lay nearby and ran to quench the flames, but the flames escalated instead. As two students dashed off to seek assistance, Taylor hoped for a miracle when he grabbed a nearby fire extinguisher, pulled the pin, and aimed it at the fire. Then he squeezed the handle and waited for a blast of powder. Nada. Zilch. Nothing! He saw his life pass before him in a heartbeat as flames began to engulf the trailer. There was one last attempt to isolate the fire and score a victory. Both students, along with Mr. Swanson, tried in vain to push the trailer outside. Nice effort but it failed miserably. They had already crossed the threshold; that handmade float now resembled a scene from "Chariots of Fire.".

"Everyone outside, and that's an order!" clamored the auto shop teacher as he pulled the alarm alerting the student body. You could read the students' minds as they questioned the timing of what they thought was a typical fire drill. A shock of reality set in, however, when a voice was broadcast across the public address system and directed students to the gym. Smoke billowed in the distance and sirens blared from multiple directions as fire units began arriving en masse. The concerns of the student body drifted from skipping fifth period to their prized possessions going up in flames.

Once assembled, instructions were issued over the intercom advising everyone what not to do. Brusque and to the point, Mr. Rigler with his true southern accent, assured staff and students that everyone had escaped unharmed, painting words of comfort in the minds of those present. For some, it felt like having a dead weight lifted off their chest.

For Breanna, that dead weight just became a little heavier. Then, with a sense of apprehension, Mr. R. dropped a bombshell. "Nobody will be allowed to return to the AG. building, neither staff nor students." In simple terms, car keys, house keys, backpacks, clothing, homework, and, heaven forbid, cell phones became inaccessible. "That sucks," was a common phrase heard among the crowd, like squirrel chatter. Meanwhile, office telephones became a hot commodity as affected students swarmed in great numbers to Mrs. Winn's office. The exhausting task of notifying parents was underway.

Imagine for a moment a parent's reaction upon receiving the phone call that day. It probably went something like this: "Mom, the school is on fire, and I can't bring any of my stuff home because the principal won't let us go back and get it. The car keys are in my purse, can you pick me up?" I'll bet that rattled some nerves. Affected teachers were also stuck between a rock and a hard place, unable to dish out homework. That meant students could not access their books—many experienced a moment of euphoria.

Smoke poured out of that drab green building, mixing with an already gray day. These were early indicators that our auto shop could be reduced to a charred shell. We were fortunate however; the fire was easily contained, courtesy of our regional smoke eaters. The next morning, school officials surveyed the interior, and I went along for the ride. I had never witnessed a fire damage evaluation with the local fire chief and his boss from the state, so that became a first for me. Words of wisdom came from the plant manager, who simply declared, "It'll have to be repaired." This shattered the dreams of those hoping for a disaster declaration and a need for a wrecking ball. As I discovered in days to come, a career opportunity was unfolding as a major painting and renovation project loomed. The boss referred to it as job security.

Anxious students and staff returned to reclaim their personal items, abandoned but untouched by flames and presumably secured. Yes, I say presumably because society today is not what it used to be. Despite all the precautions taken, kleptomania reared its ugly head. Nothing is safe. Victimized, a handful of students sought my help, and we tried to sort things out. Those having cellular withdrawal symptoms were blissfully reunited with their devices. Then reality set in; there would be homework.

Some of the most dangerous untruths are truths marginally distorted, as was the case against Breanna. Rumors began circulating that she would need to provide a few Benjamins to help pay for the property damage. The gossip turned out to be precisely that, and everyone took pity on the poor girl. Then, there was the matter of Taylor's friend Ryan, understandably miffed. Yes, if you had planned to watch your girlfriends on a parade float and your display was cremated, that would alter your lifestyle dramatically. Taylor and his friend Ryan had worked countless hours repairing and refurbishing their Ford Mustang. After all that hard work and sweat labor, the parade float was reduced to a charred shell. It seems to me, if memories are all that remain, there is a story the boys can tell their grandkids someday. Ditto for Breanna. She decided auto repair was not her cup of tea and turned to phlebotomy.

THE WIRELESS RAGE

Most of the world is currently experiencing a pandemic, specifically a technology pandemic, initiated by one of the most prominent methods of communication. Cellular phone usage has exploded in recent years. More than two-thirds of the globe has connected to one carrier or another, based on 2010 estimates. Notice I use the word "pandemic," because it continues to spread. And we still have a long way to go before it reaches its peak. It's virtually unstoppable. Do you remember lining up for concert tickets? Now people camp out for the newest release of a wireless application. This cell-phone craze is becoming the rage on every street corner and across school campuses, creating talkaholics and textaholics around the globe. Our rural school is no exception.

Not long ago, children were required to phone home using a payphone. Remember E.T.? Today parents are absorbed in their child's sporting events, traveling multiple directions while watching their fuel evaporate. An impromptu call is all that is needed to help retain their sanity, and monitoring the kids with a cell phone is justifiable. In my day we were monitored by the sun. "Be home before dark," Mom would say. For those grounded students complaining they need to chat with their friends, I say: get over it.

Do you remember passing notes? Now teens are too busy texting and conversing with anyone, even those who just happen to be down the hallway. Sure, it's not my phone, but what a waste of minutes, and when the bill arrives, it'll be time to hock the jewelry. How students can afford it during these tough economic times is a topic for discussion. Some have it all figured out, however. Take Emily for example, a teen moocher. I overheard Emily brag to her friend Amanda, "My cell phone bill is two hundred bucks." "OMG, Emily, how are you going to pay for it?" quipped Amanda. "Mom's going to take care of it," Emily snapped back. Good ole Mom. Sounds like a bailout plan to me.

Here's my opinion on students and cell phones, and it is likely to be as popular as brussels sprout on a school lunch menu. There are too many students using the 24/7 anytime/anywhere plan. As I stumble into their conversations, invading their space, I discover the truth. We are creatures of habit. Give teens (mostly girls) a phone, and as sure as the price of gas rises, they will be talking anytime they want, anywhere they want, as long as they are not caught. Usually the

VP *will* catch them in the act, and then exert his power and authority to confiscate that cherished wireless gadget. By waiting till the end of the day to return it, he has saved the user precious minutes. Repeat violators, who refuse to play by the rules, may find their cell phones in the hands of their parents, with a consequence attached.

In the grand scheme of events, how does this affect me or where do I fit in? What is the cell phone connection between the student and custodian?

Check this out.

Try walking across the parking lot while a student is driving and talking on the phone simultaneously. You see this played out on your city streets daily. They will tear around a blind corner on two wheels, and should you happen to be in their path, its body slam, baby! Famous or defunct notables have streets and intersections named after them, but I have no plans to have a sign erected in my honor. Some states have enacted strict laws regarding driving and talking or texting. Regardless, I always recommend updating those life insurance policies anyway.

If that isn't enough for you, try to outrun the camera phones. Those elusive objects will forever capture you when you least expect it. Avoiding them requires some fancy footwork, particularly with five extra pounds of metal hanging from my belt. Once, I was caught in the crossfire of camera phone flash. It reminded me of those notorious paparazzi photo shoots. I have heard stories about teachers who became infamous stars on the Internet through no fault of their own. Even student brawls (whether real or staged) have been recorded for your viewing pleasure and possibly some recognition for the cast.

Tanya and Erika, two aspiring actresses, starred in one such episode of their own, courtesy of YouTube. Their phony encounter produced some fanfare; however, not a drop of blood could be found at the scene. Having known the duo, I questioned their intentions, which appeared rather jejune. "We just wanted our five minutes of fame," they said. It became their meteoric film career. Whether on the big screen or your HDTV, the promotion of hostilities has escalated. Ladies, there are other ways to get attention; trust me. Violence, whether real or imagined, simply promotes more violence.

This cell phone madness is responsible for other bizarre events that occurred during my custodial career. Whenever a student loses an expensive personal item, e.g. car keys with a computer chip, cameras, or cell phones, they approach me in a panic, expecting me to perform magic. Yet another event occurs, more frequently, that will blow you away. Their prized possessions magically reappear in another student's locker. Sometimes they are never seen again, and sometimes it's *why* they're never seen again that is sure to entertain you.

Katelyn was a towering young lady, a basketball jock. It was her positive disposition however, that allowed her to rise above all obstacles. A fair-skinned brunette, this junior was a popular teaching assistant who always managed to finish a teacher's task, even at the eleventh hour. Her charming personality melted hearts like the warm sun on the early morning frost. However, this agile young lady was prone to two unfortunate habits. She enjoyed wandering the halls when she ran errands for a teacher. And she was constantly preoccupied which played a pivotal role in the loss of personal items, including her cell phone.

One day, after an hour of endless searching for me, Katelyn and I had a chance encounter in the hallway, where she pleaded with me to retrieve her phone for the second time. She stated emphatically the unusual circumstances surrounding her phone's disappearance. As Kate was finishing her personal business in the restroom, the cell phone slipped out of her coat pocket and fell directly into the toilet. Recovering it, well, that was another matter. Katelyn asked me, "Can you find it?" As I stated before, I have retrieved an assortment of items out of the johns; why would this episode be any different? Then I remembered, I work in a school and no two days are alike. I was certain of that, just as I was certain the functions of the cell phone would be nonexistent. All I needed were the large green gloves, and the recovery project would be underway.

As we approached the restroom, I located a "Closed" sign and positioned it in the doorway to keep all the Looky Lou's out. Then I sent Katelyn inside to make sure all was clear and extricate any potential campers. Before I entered, I asked her a specific question. "It's still lying on the bottom of the toilet, right?" She said, "No, I already flushed it." After a long pause and holding back the laughter, I informed Katelyn that her cell phone was most likely halfway down the septic line. Yet, to fulfill my custodial duties, I still needed to perform the inspection. After examining each individual toilet, I found every one to be clear and free of any object. The situation was evolving from a drama to a comedy, and it was time to issue a progress report. Miss Schroeder, please advise your mom that your cell phone is history. There is no chance it will return, and hopefully it will clear our septic system.

The impact of losing two cell phones over a brief period was not as devastating a blow to Katelyn as I had anticipated. Some girls have cried a river over a lost ten-dollar piece of jewelry, but not our Katelyn. There was no hint of a tear and no drama queen; she accepted the loss rather nonchalantly, as if it were an everyday occurrence. Little did I know after a few months passed, Kate would soon own her third cell phone. Yes, her third cell phone. Whether she was forgetful in nature or preoccupied, I had no answer. All I knew was, her prized possession was tubing down the pipes, and Katelyn was probably rehearsing the spiel she would deliver to Mom when she arrived home. Contrasting her situation, Mr. Weatherford, our vice principal, continued to add more wireless objects to his daily mounting collection. Just think of the unlimited calling time the habitual offenders could provide him if it was legal.

With less than two hours until the final bell, cleanup evolved into the *Amazing Race*. In one week, those munchkins produce a truckload of trash and enough waste to bury a schoolbus. Then I found a cluster of wadded papers in the hallway and wondered why they were there. The trash can was just a few feet away. I know, that's asking too much. Curiosity got the best of me, and I decided to open the papers to see if someone had left their name at the top. I could always have it hand-delivered to one of their classes by a teacher's aide as a lesson in responsibility, and to create a moment of embarrassment. What I discovered were love notes of a sexual nature—with names listed, no less. There is enough smut in circulation today; do we need more? It was time for the censor to dispose of this explicit material before virgin souls were corrupted. Someone was not exactly the sharpest tack on the wall. As you can see, if it doesn't eventually arrive in the trash can, it will become general information for the free world.

The Mysterious Canteen

Tracking down hidden alcohol and drugs on the school campus is not in my job description. If, however, that is what you have been asked, then it requires some quick-witted investigating, unless your presence is graced with drug sniffing canines.

"Keep a watchful eye out for a suspicious individual," was Mr. Weatherford's impassioned plea. Breakfast was underway and I could just imagine someone sneaking through the line with a bottle of Jack Daniels tucked away in a backpack. You never know what's being smuggled into school. Naturally, it would be helpful to access additional information regarding this suspect. What comes to mind are exotic hair colors, noticeable quirks, inebriated speech, or anything that would make the individual conspicuous like Aunt Martha's intoxicating perfume inside an elevator. Mr. Weatherford continued, "I don't have a description of this person, and what little I do know is based on sketchy information. He may decide to make an appearance in the cafeteria." We were clueless regarding what this kid looked like, more or less grasping at straws. We didn't even know what this person's gender was. I wondered what popular sleuth we should have consulted for this case. Columbo? The solitary clue we had was that this person had a canteen, if we could only get our hands on it.

I thought to myself facetiously, *That definitely narrows it down.* "Not a problem," I responded. "I will alert the kitchen staff as well. You never know if this kid will pull a fast one and spike the food. (Visions of Eddie (the bad boy) reappearing to torment us began to materialize. Instead of chewing gum, this joker could add a little John Barleycorn to the fruit cocktail. Who would be better qualified?) Mr. Weatherford agreed with my idea on a whim and muttered, "May be sending one student home today."

On that note, I still needed to perform my civic duty, reminding everyone that school was in session. With a reassuring smile, this stern V.P. decided to return to his office, greeted by Mrs. Winn and a stack of referrals piled on his desk. Yes, it goes with the territory.

I returned to the cafeteria, and much to my chagrin, I discovered the remains of a flattened milk carton. Nothing new; it was the same childish, immature prank, occurring on a different day. The timing was impeccable, however, as I observed a student displaying unusual behavior. He fumbled with his backpack in the distance, appearing as guilty as a child caught with his hand in the cookie jar. Perhaps that is one reason backpacks are considered taboo among law enforcement. Whom do you trust? I approached the kid, like a cat about to pounce, when a staff member emerged from the kitchen and began to interrogate him. Eventually he relinquished, seemingly unconcerned, and delivered a Leatherman, nothing more. Was that it? No drugs, no alcohol? Surely something was amiss, or the great deception had just occurred.

Like bears awakening from hibernation, students began arriving on the buses and storming the kitchen as breakfast was being served. "Sup?" asked a student while carrying his breakfast tray, consisting of a chocolate donut and milk. "What it is?" replied his best friend, hoping to get a taste of the pastry. Question any student, it was their favorite entrée of the week, sold every Friday until the nutrition police put the lid on that program. Regardless of the regulations, there is no law in the books prohibiting students from bringing their own pastries to circumvent the system. Not one seat was available in the house that day. It was wall to wall.

Five minutes had elapsed when I returned to the lunchroom, escorting a mop bucket with a broken wheel to a central location. Screech! While en route, I randomly observed the floors for vitamin D puddles and jettisoned cocoa puffs, while primed to make an announcement. "Your mother doesn't work here, pick it up." That shady-looking middle school student was still stuffing his face, like a skid-row bum in a steak house planning to dine and dash. Out of the corner of my eye, I saw an interesting situation unfolding. One of our high school students was passing around a flask and allowing others to inhale it like dollar-store perfume. Could it be the same bottle the staff was investigating? All bets were on. The bottle was proving to be a hit with students, so I decided to pursue it further.

I tried to avoid Nathan, a hard rocker with shoulder-length hair. Nice kid, but you could not escape his conversations. He usually wore headphones, blaring to the sounds of grunge rock and will likely be fitted with a hearing aid by the time he is thirty. For the moment, I was the only adult in the immediate area, trying to multitask by observing two people and performing crowd control. That was a trick in itself when you consider the hundreds of students wolfing down a weekly dose of pastry. I pleaded, "Don't forget your trash," but the minute I turned my head, a table of eight scattered like quail. It was me against the world, and the odds weren't in my favor.

I tried not to appear too suspicious by leaving some breathing room between us, but that failed miserably. I was losing sight of the suspect, who managed to elude me and anyone that she felt was invading her space. As the hour approached ten minutes before bell time, navigating the halls nearly required a bullhorn to cut through the assembled mob. My face almost met the concrete when I tripped on someone's feet protruding in the aisle. The elusive girl vanished, as if anticipating a possible search and seizure, which brought further speculation; the water bottle must have been in her possession. Slim chance I'd ever see it again.

The lunchroom chatter was slowly progressing in my direction, ever increasing in volume and giving me the impression I was enclosed in an aviary. From out of nowhere, a thin, dark-haired figure emerged. Like a magnet, Jenna attracted a throng of followers. Everyone wanted to be her friend, but for all the wrong reasons. I asked her point-blank, "Jenna, what can you tell me about a canteen that's popular with the students?" She replied, "It's in my locker."

"Really? I asked." Without hesitation, she agreed to allow me the pleasure of escorting her to the evidence.

There was something wrong with this picture. I thought she had devised a scheme and I was playing into her hands. As we approached her locker, it occurred to me that many students would refuse to discuss the matter, period. I watched Jenna play with the locker combination like a professional safecracker, biding her time. Eventually, the door opened with a spine-chilling squeak befitting some haunted dwelling. That door definitely needs WD-40.

The freshman reached inside and grabbed the canteen in question. Without hesitation, she delivered it to me while claiming she was only storing it at the request of another student. Painstakingly, I unscrewed the lid and took a whiff for myself: beer. It was exactly what my investigative instincts had dictated from day one. This young woman was storing alcohol, and it was unknown how many students had sampled it. Only reliable breathalyzers could make that determination. "I think you had better come with me to the principal's office," I informed her. "No problem," she replied. The stroll back to the office was interesting, perhaps a bit perplexing. The under-aged booze provider advised me she had a story to tell our curious vice principal, and a chair was reserved in her name in Mr. Weatherford's office.

Days passed and I never saw the young lady return, nor did I see the kid with the Leatherman. They were quite the odd couple. After consulting with Mr. Weatherford, I found out their stories had disintegrated upon cross-examination. It's kind of like leaving your wallet at the scene of the crime. So, there is reason to be suspicious if you see your fellow student sharing that forty-four-ounce fountain drink with his homies. It could be a beverage modified for their inebriating pleasure.

IN MEMORY

"Children seldom have a proper sense of their own tragedy, discounting and keeping hidden the true horrors of their short lives, humbly imagining real calamity to be some prestigious drama of the grown-up world," says American author Shirley Hazzard. This quotation with a powerful message is frequently overlooked and often misunderstood. For many of us, it resonates deep within our hearts, specifically parents, grandparents and all who have suffered a loss. The somber truth remains, there is always a child who is vulnerable to danger, has a natural attraction to it, and may fail to recognize the imminent threat before its occurrence.

Today's teens face ever-increasing quandaries: peer pressure, teen parenting, alcohol and drug abuse, cyberbullying, and a multitude of physical and psychological issues. This can result from a potpourri of family situations, some of which are unavoidable. It is nothing short of a miracle how children manage to survive a dysfunctional home life, such as when a domestic situation places them in protective custody. It's a full plate, even for the most stalwart. As you gradually become acquainted with these students, it is as if you have known them like family. Some will writhe with emotional pain and spill their guts to any listening audience.

Everyone has a story to tell, and some of their renditions are tantamount to heartbreak. Over the years, students trials and tribulations have been rekindled, while we the audience tried to absorb the anguish that befell them. I've seen the fear and experienced the sorrow. Yes, even the mighty oak can only endure so much. While every situation varies by degree, each student bears his or her own private suffering in some way. Some may feel isolated and assume a fetal position, or they may simply wish to be left alone. Others may lash out at the establishment, claiming they are not being heard or understood by adults. Whatever the situation, you may become the unintentional psychologist when they finally decide to tell their story.

Here's a lamentable fact to ponder: a small, yet significant percentage of today's teens will not live to see their twenty-first birthday. Our high school has experienced this unforeseen tragedy on several occasions. While the incidents may vary, the pain is real, affecting both staff and students. Trying to convince a majority of teens they are not invincible is counter-intuitive. How could we forget we were once in their shoes? Let us simply remember that life is precious at any age.

Before the legendary pop duo Jan and Dean sang their rendition of "Dead Man's Curve," Jan Berry must have given some forethought prior to writing the song. It's a timeless classic, and an unfortunate reality for our high school, and probably yours. Less than two miles from our campus, a tree is adorned with a memorial as a testament to those lyrics and signifying Kenny's premature departure. Let us not forget Matt and Billy; we miss you as well. Regardless of the decade, the 50s or the 90s, the result is the same. For whatever reason, known or unknown, a driver failed to negotiate a curve. The list is endless and eternal.

The world was a better place when Ryan, one of our gifted athletes, displayed his talents as a competitive long distance runner. As a sport that is often overlooked due to the status and hype of football and basketball, track retains its own niche. Make no mistake; track and field maintains a continuous diehard fan base with loyal followers.

Ryan had hopes and dreams just as much as any teenager, and was well liked by fellow students and staff. His coach held him in high esteem for his athleticism and integrity. Not simply satisfied with sports, he also possessed a fondness for and allegiance to the Boy Scouts, whom he served proudly. Both occupied and fulfilled his earthly time.

Ryan's demise came as a devastating blow to the student body, and particularly his coach and trainers. A memorial service was held in our high school gym before a capacity crowd of mourners, including fellow scouts, classmates, and those who knew this model student. An emotional eulogy spoken by our Track coach stirred memories of a student who had become an overachiever in his field and whose future had looked promising. That moment in time became unsurpassed when our Boy Scout received a tribute befitting a dignitary. Facing the casket, the scoutmaster delivered a somber and formal closing Boy Scout salute. There was scarcely a dry eye in the building when the words were uttered, "Ryan, job well done." Ryan has been elevated to angel scout.

Perhaps your school district, your employees, or your family members or circle of friends have experienced an incident of this caliber. I know the pain you have endured. The suffering is real and permeates the central core of your inner being. I extend my heartfelt empathy to you. For those who are indifferent to the families who have suffered tragedies of this proportion, you simply do not comprehend the fact that children remain our most precious commodity.

Parents, savor the moments you spend quality time with your sons and daughters. They grow up in the blink of an eye, and when you think they have become a burden, they are gone. For some, it's packing up and heading off to college. For others, it's tying the knot and starting a family. The home suddenly incurs a deathly silence, and you find yourself a victim of the empty nest syndrome.

JUST ANOTHER DAY

It was barely twenty-five minutes on the upside of eight, and red-eyed, caffeine-seeking students who'd burned the midnight oil listening to their iPods were hammering the soda machines. Like desperate gamblers feeding their last dollar into the slots, some failed to read the fine print: use correct change only. I will emphasize that these are dollar slots and not change machines for the big bucks. If, however, students still felt a need to waste those greenbacks, I am certain the beverage company would always be elated with the additional earnings.

It was time to meander to the high school's main office, wearing my yellow slicker, reminiscent of a popular fisherman. Instantly, I became the subject of an amusing discussion, due to my disheveled appearance. You see, Evergreen Valley High was built smack in the middle of a windtunnel; or so it seemed. Call it Mother Nature's love affair with our facial countenance; it gave greater perception to a bad hair day. We agreed that everyone accepted this weather phenomenon reluctantly. Our high society Alisha, with eye shadow flowing down her cheeks, could be heard whining incessantly.

After the office merriment had subsided, the conversation altered mid-stream to the condition of the flags to be raised. Questioning Mrs. Kinney, I emphasized that the tattered one was in dire need of replacement. She agreed. With luck, there would be a spare tucked away amid the clutter hidden in the vault. If not, it would be time to call 1-800-BuyFlag.

Old Glory was unfurled, and, thankfully, there was no audience on hand when I realized this flag might never make it up the pole. Some jackass was deliberately playing the devil with me by tying the rope into a cluster of loops and twists. What was the point? It was obvious someone had intended to make my life hell by creating this conundrum. I struggled valiantly, and occasionally scanned the area for any practical joker hiding behind a vehicle, snickering. Perhaps it was a nightshift employee bored with his job, or maybe a vengeful student messing with me. I would have returned the favor until I realized this might evolve into an endless, mindless game with no winners and more roadblocks awaiting next time.

I had no hands free to answer when my two-way radio began blurting out my number repeatedly as the flag finally made its way to the top. Mrs. McKinley, our middle school secretary, had become impatient and called maintenance in desperation. Like everyone else, she would need to wait. Presumably, some kid had puked. They do that a lot, you know. This time, Lady Luck prevailed, and I breathed a sigh of relief. A recently enrolled student had encountered a zipper quandary with his jacket. According to Mrs. McKinley, it would require some of my "magic." Magic?

I imagined what I could accomplish with that capability, and the possibilities were endless. The secretary's efforts to solve the zipper crisis proved futile, while mine were successful. Thanks to my unorganized tool cart containing every item thinkable—except those that had recently been jacked—I performed the delicate procedure that morning. It started as progressive tinkering, but eventually I exceeded the student's every expectation and, oddly enough, my own. The kid was happy, that's all that mattered. And you can't make everyone happy, as was the case with a griping mother, who met me in the cafeteria.

Listening to a parent complain about her lethargic child's inability to respond to wake-up requests is not the way I usually start my day. This mom had a lot of steam to blow off, and apparently I was the relief valve. Imagine that parental predicament amplified when the student resets the snooze alarm between their first and third period classes. Their somnolence is evident as they enter the cafeteria with that zombie look.

I remember some early mornings that I spent in despair while attempting to rouse my son, who could sleep through an earthquake. I brought a phonograph into his room one morning and commenced playing 78 rpm records. The tango was effective because it was annoying and prolonged. *Reveille,* in its clamorousness, usually meant mission accomplished.

The first day back from winter break disappointed one lanky sophomore sporting an ear stud. His arrogant attitude progressed to a near requirement for anger management counseling. As he pummeled the pop machine, it simply ignored his pounding fist and accompanying stream of expletives (which I have deleted here). The beverage dispenser obstinately refused to yield. Taking matters into his own hands, this student with the 80s hairdo shook and coerced the vending machine to his satisfaction. He stopped briefly to hear my lecture, as I explained in vivid detail his potential physical appearance should the metal contraption fall on him. He reflected for a moment, then resumed his tirade, ignoring me. Sign up this bad boy as a future entrant to the University of Clueless. Welcome to the real world, kid. Just down the hall and around the corner, two female students wearing non-dress-code, exceedingly provocative attire sipped on their blended iced coffee of choice. They were capturing all the attention their little hearts desired. Walking through a maze of male students, I encountered the girls on my way to the main office. Amid the confusion and distraction, a conversation materialized regarding their drinks. Neither rain nor the winter's chill would prohibit these young women from enjoying their perennial favorite. When the weather moderated, I indulged as well; however, I do not feel the need for self-induced brain freeze when a climatic one suffices.

Our glamour girls continued to parade through the halls, making a fashion statement and utilizing the form of advertising they knew best. Both were absorbed in their own little worlds, about to meet their waterloo. The enforcer of dress codes, Mr. Weatherford, and the girls were on a collision course. I knew the results of that meeting when they arrived at Mrs. Winn's office. Those smiles that once decorated their faces evaporated. By contrast, my expectations were high; the kitchen staff had made a fresh pot of coffee and awaited my return. While it was impossible to surpass Espresso Girls (my coffee klatsch), drinking the kitchen's coffee was the best method to take advantage of a depleted budget and still receive a free caffeine jolt.

I returned to the mess hall, (our cafeteria), where science studies could monitor eating habits. The second bell resonated its irrefutable ring for all, except those skipping class. Students that were caught wandering the halls concluded, for whatever reason, that they were exempt from referrals. Their stories displayed apathy upon questioning. The procrastinators met with Mr. Weatherford, who has probably heard every excuse in the book regarding "why I'm late for class." The vice principal needed some snappy retorts to keep his sanity. "Third time this week, Joey, and it's only Monday." There were days the entrance to his office resembled the checkout line at 7-Eleven.

I was enjoying a moment of serenity until a well-meaning teacher's aide seized my attention and revealed the latest childish episode, performed in the freshman hallway. From all indications, it appeared someone had drop-kicked a container of yogurt about three times, giving the floor a rainbow appearance. To add insult to injury, they had also painted a mural on the wall with the yogurt, so I would not get bored. Their lack of artistic skills told me they were probably not enrolled in art class, and their graffiti art would eventually give them away. How thoughtful of these individuals, trying to do their best to keep my job secure. Surprisingly, it seemed to be working.

In my absence, those preoccupied kitchen ladies found themselves role-playing the cooks' version of *Survivor*. A hasty resolution meant the difference between a smooth transition, or food prep in *Hell's Kitchen*. It became necessary to generate a last-minute menu change, requiring me to alter my work schedule and enter the freezer. By chance, I wore the perfect T-shirt for that occasion. The comment, "Let me drop everything and work on your problem," caught the attention of various staff. You need a sense of humor in this job, or risk going crazy.

The cooks' request to locate additional ground beef, was more of a demand, but in a tactfully delightful way. The excavation out in cold storage was painfully slow and futile as I searched for something that no longer existed. Ten brutal minutes of fruitless exploring in a below-zero environment constitutes cruel and unusual punishment. Once I realized the supply was depleted and a bone-chilling numbness had set in, I presented the kitchen ladies with another dilemma. "Do you have a backup plan?" I asked.

Those greasy burger patties were so popular last week that we have run out. Why not serve some healthy hot dogs? "I don't think they make healthy hot dogs," laughed one of the cooks. Following a lengthy debate, the filler selected was the standard PB&J sandwich, making everyone's day. There were no more trips to the icebox; a place that only penguins and polar bears could love.

The termination of first period signaled an end to tranquility. Teenagers, with their voracious appetites, made a beeline for the student square, the location of the highly acclaimed snack bar. Sneaking through the back hall to avoid the crush, I met Roy, our math teacher, from the opposite direction, and we encountered two couples lip locked. As we converged, one pair rolled their eyes in defiance and dispersed. The other two, however, remained embraced while we drew a crowd for their benefit. "Let's all gather round for a nice group hug," we chimed in unison. That was enough to burst their bubble and send them packing.

The aroma of recently baked chocolate chip cookies wafting from the snack bar beckoned and represented a superlative method of sales advertising. As usual, they flew off the shelf. Those late arrivals with a sweet tooth were left with only unfilled hopes. Short on change, a persistent female student sporting jet-black hair and excessive makeup badgered me into donating a dollar for her cause. There was something about her face that struck me. She appeared primed for the mosh pit, not fourth period. "Sorry, I had a dollar yesterday, but I spent it before arriving to work." I told her I needed a caffeine boost to make it through the morning. Discouraged, she wandered off, a failed deception. It was the same young lady panhandling once again, for the third time that week.

Fast forward to twelve thirty. Silence is golden. The completion of high school lunch signals the inception of empty halls and a deserted lunchroom. In exchange for the serenity, however, the students marked their territory before they dispersed. It's a sight, guaranteed to take your breath away. The first thing I noticed was a brown pond behind a table, created by a massive cola spill. As a bonus, there was broken glass and unidentifiable liquids partially hidden under a booth that radiated a hint of perfume. Adding insult to injury, I stepped into a pile of noodles and sauce where someone had crashed and burned. After passing through this pigpen, I asked myself, *Is this high school or daycare?*

INFESTATIONS

The attendance secretary's gag reflexes tend to have a short life span. Ditto for most everyone I know. That said, I highly recommend sending a sickly student home ASAP before the cleanup evolves into a domino effect. If Ashley becomes ill while her parents are working, someone must render a decision regarding who is going to retrieve her. School staff (especially the janitor) always appreciates punctuality if the situation involves a fever or rash, or the child's head hovering over the wastebasket. Grandma, Uncle Bob, or the reluctant big sister could receive that spontaneous phone call, as long as they are on the list. We have no preference, which taxi service will pick up and deliver.

Valid parental concerns are always on our mind when our teenagers leave for school. Yet, those distressing anxieties may not materialize until our offspring arrive home ill or ready to engage in battle. Sports conflicts, teacher conferences, suspension notices, and a major health crisis are but a few decisive reasons for an investment in a school year's supply of acid reducers and pain relievers. For those who are slightly balding or subject to premature graying, welcome to the club.

If I mention the words "your child" and "head lice" together in the same sentence, what should be a parent's initial response? Perhaps going postal, followed by a NASCAR run to their neighborhood drugstore would not be inconceivable. This age-old parasitic, wingless insect of the order *Anoplura* has given a multitude of families a close encounter of the worst kind. Not only is it time-consuming, it tests your tolerance and restraint levels. Picking those sticky little nits out of your child's hair is not exactly how you ever plan to spend your day off from work. In the face of adversity, it is best to prepare, and I would recommend a small investment—latex gloves and a magnifying glass.

Any school (regardless of its demographics) is prone to an outbreak at some point in history. There is little chance of dodging a bullet, and we endured our moment, which kept all of the secretaries and many of our staff performing a thankless job. Unfortunately, our middle school became a hotbed of critter reproduction. Desks, books, bedding, clothing, and you name it all required sanitizing or laundering. A commission was appointed (of which I was the lone member) to consistently perform those time-consuming duties. Meanwhile, the washer and dryer operated 24/7 to keep up with this nightmare. What I failed to finish during the day was done at night by our dedicated night watchman. The green gloves were a godsend as I piled the infested clothing into a plastic bag and placed it inside a shopping cart for immediate sterilization. We spared nothing. With the health authorities issuing their mandates for elimination, the district could not risk one slimy critter slipping through the cracks. Based on a recent eradication attempt with a dismal success rate, I pitched everything in the washer, slammed the door shut, and began destroying the evidence.

If you're a baby boomer, you probably remember those lengthy inoculation lines back in the 60s. We approached that level when each class was summoned to report for a health screening. Fearing the worst, children fidgeted while standing pell-mell outside the attendance office, anxiously awaiting their turn as the staff donned surgical gloves. For the brave secretaries involved, this was an exhausting procedure. Countless hours were consumed. Secretarial skills that could have been utilized, were devoted instead to sifting through hair strands ranging from the buzz cut to the mohawk and everything in between. Every child's head was transformed into a critter breeding ground, and parents' phones rang off the hook with grim incoming messages.

The ambience changed dramatically upon re-entering the attendance office. The area resembled an exam room while Mrs. McKinley and her assistants performed reenactments from the TV show *Scrubs*. "More germicidal and more gloves, please!" came the cries from this office. The parasitic battle was a race against time. I became the nurses assistant in my own right, constantly running for supplies and trying to keep up with the demand. The staff emptied boxes of gloves and consumed spray bottles (filled with a mysterious potion) the way little girls go through lipstick.

The eradication continued, and the secretaries appeared to be on the verge of winning the war against the infestation. While their mission was nearing completion, mine was work in progress. The need for my janitorial expertise was in demand by school personnel, and in a unique fashion. Donning a white jumpsuit, mask, and hairnet, I bore a resemblance to those 1950s sci-fi lab technicians. While the protection was overkill and a tad daunting, I instantly became fodder for gossip. Their crisis was a plea to disinfect the interior of a company vehicle from top to bottom. I guess I couldn't blame them for taking these precautions.

So how did our school end up in this miserable situation to begin with? An employee was assigned to pick up a student at the child's residence, due to transportation issues. After returning to the school, the employee noticed something crawling on the headrest of the car seat. She soon discovered that the passenger's hair was teeming with those nasty nits. While collecting a mélange of the passenger's items, the employee came into close contact with the infected person. The rest is history, as we say.

It was simply a matter of time before additional infestations blossomed, and a few casual references to the plague were overheard. Rumor had it one of our office personnel became emotional and began carrying on like a blind dog in a meat market. Hey, it's a school for crying out loud; these events are inevitable. Who would be the next victim of this louse invasion? Now we had staff examining each other's hair, and the mere mention of the word "lice" brought glares from anyone involved.

ASSEMBLIES AND DANCES

Unlike the innocuous and subdued pep assemblies of yesteryear, today's rambunctious, choreographic cheerleaders and their male counterparts provide blockbuster entertainment. High school assemblies were pretty tame in my day. Now, films such as *Bring it On* give new meaning and new life to cheerleading. Not only is it a sport, it has become an aerial performance. There are more thrills and spills (emphasis on spills) than Barnum and Bailey's Big Top.

In our school, once the show was concluded, the aftermath was ubiquitous and yielded all the incriminating evidence for assembly attendees to observe. The cheerleaders' failure to furnish adequate cover for the gymnasium floor could only beg the question: what were they thinking? Student-body mishaps fluctuated depending on the theme of the week. Varying from shaving cream to a facsimile of maple syrup spills (uniquely created by puddles of dried soda pop) everything was detrimental. A broad spectrum of potentially damaging fluids decorated the hardwood floor despite repeated admonitions.

There was a genuine feeling of uneasiness when I distributed a roll of duct tape to some of our aspiring cheer squad. Perhaps it was those sad, wanting eyes seasoned with a sugar-coated "please" that convinced me to relinquish that roll. When I returned, to my horror and dismay, I found the gym floor resembling a giant patchwork quilt. And since hardwoods do not take kindly to adhesives, the combination of foot traffic and building heat is synonymous to melting chewing gum on hot pavement. Once the cheerleaders had completed their performance, the burden to restore the floor was the next act.

As you would probably expect, administrators requested those who created this sad state of affairs to remain and assist me in refurbishing the decimated parquet. Most did not mind the thought of missing their next class period. But soon they learned of their fate and what they were required to do, which provided them every excuse to depart prematurely. It was time to apply elbow grease while incorporating a degree of patience, something student's lack. These were the key ingredients necessary for the hardwood revival. There was also some chanting that occurred, since it was my elbow going through the motions that brought the luster back.

One day, and for what seemed like an eternity thereafter, arms flailed and bodies boogied when the world became infatuated with a phenomenon simply titled the "Macarena." With its catchy, repetitious chorus, this infectious dance craze (the greatest since the Twist) manifested itself in night clubs, dance halls, and high schools around the globe. We were not the exception, and we capitalized on the moment. Most staff members didn't mind the exuberance and ostensibly childlike innocence of this passing fad, since everyone and their Uncle Joe wanted to get into the act. Hey, even I was sucked into the one-hit wonder as the student council incorporated the dance as part of the coming assembly.

The "Macarena" would enter the record books for longevity, but would soon become only a memory for the dance team and their audiences. When the curtain came down on this musical craze, the replacement was an abrupt 180 for parents and the staff. Following on its heels, the loathsome gangsta rap and its obscene lyrics were mutually united with an erotic dance movement. This illicit activity repulsed both the staff and chaperones, who searched for a solution short of canceling all the hip-hop events.

Some students cried foul, because for them the dance was the highlight of the week. It all came down to Mr. Rigler's final answer; The Big Kahuna called the shots.

Sure, I had an ounce of empathy for the kids, but it wasn't my call. I preferred the simplicity of the past. Just give me some knee-slapping, foot-stomping 60s doo-wop accompanied by some amazing vocals and that will surely draw a receptive crowd.

As the warm spring-like weather finally made its debut, it seemed to conflict with an archaic and often temperamental boiler. Preparing for weekend dances frequently required altering the climate in the building. Staff strategically positioned *ginormous* fans for air movement and to control body odor, as the cafeteria gradually began to morph into a locker-room environment. Those crowd-arousing fog machines at rock shows would have provided some desperately needed air circulation. But not to worry. We had yet to exceed the DEQ's air-quality alert status, thanks to an invention called "scented air fresheners." The dance-floor atmosphere became chaperone-friendly once again, complements of a potent marvel in an aerosol can.

Depending on the year and the behavior patterns of the students, it was either feast or famine when it came down to the number of dances held. During one of our busy years, I was drafted in desperation to chaperone. By acting in loco parentis, my presence was a key factor in avoiding a cancellation. As a surrogate parent, I constantly monitored couples that chose to venture outside for fresh air. Of course, others preferred various forms of illegal entertainment. By comparison, it made some of us baby boomers appear to be the saints we were not.

Recently, a new dance criterion was given full administrative blessings in order to restore some dignity to this antiquated form of social expression. Like the vexatious radio commercial that reminds us, "You'll be sorry," if you make another choice, we gave students only one dancing option. The staff was beaming from ear to ear. The once necessary fire extinguishers, primed to cool off flaming hot dance partners, now sat idle in their respective cabinets. New regulations were recently implemented to provide all chaperones a needed advantage: face-to-face, one-inch space.

Not long ago, students were allowed to access their lockers during dances, albeit this would allow them to disappear from the watchful eye of the chaperone. Somewhere in the annals of recorded school incidents is the story of a student who returned to the dance floor progressively inebriated. Classmates began to notice that Macy's conversations were off-the-wall and breathless, and she appeared somewhat disheveled. An administrator was alerted and suspected someone had smuggled in a bottle of hooch, thus a locker search was initiated. That bottle of Jack Daniels was easily accessible and, I should add, self-incriminating evidence. For this brown-eyed imbiber, it guaranteed a free ride off school property. Within minutes, the men in blue came calling and whisked her away, and her absence was duly noted.

MEMORABLE MOMENTS

There exists today an adverse view of our emerging young-adult population, much of which can be attributed to an increasing crime rate. This makes it difficult for the public to give credit, where credit is due. All it takes is one malefactor to ruin it for the rest of those meritorious high school students. Our wayward sons and daughters receive ample publicity for their errant schemes. Why give them more recognition than they deserve? Furthermore, the glaring eyes of the populace view many of our facilities as boarding schools rather than learning establishments. Being optimistic, I still believe the achievers outnumber those who prefer to go along for a free ride. I am referring to those aspiring young scholars who strive to maintain a respectable GPA and are members of the National Honor Society. These top-notch students are often taken for granted, like photo albums. Occasionally, we will dust them off and admire them for a few minutes before they are stowed away, only to become a memory. Going the extra mile, these academic winners receive a high five in my book.

This brings me to a personal acknowledgement of one individual who fulfilled her educational duties in high school. I wish to focus on a young woman that deserves recognition and hopefully continued to pursue her wishes. She was not simply a model student, but a well-respected member of the school community. Her charming personality was enchanting and her warm smile, comforting. All of this paled by comparison to the unforgettable words she once spoke about me. These words would translate into soothing medicine during the course of the evening.

I watched Christine grow and mature in middle school accompanied by an inquisitive group of comrades who always seemed to have questions to ask. Though somewhat reticent compared to her peers, when she did speak, the world would listen. And persistent! How could I say "no" to those dark brown eyes? From Band-Aids to yearbook autographs, to a smattering of paternal advice, I disbursed a potpourri of everything relevant to the moment. Christine was always satisfied with the results, whether tangible or not. Never did she once hesitate to display her talent as a band musician and concert choir singer. Moreover, when she requested my presence at various music recitals, without hesitation, I accepted her invitations. Little did I realize she would save the best for last.

An unusually tepid spring evening greeted us as the National Honor Society hosted a dessert and social in the high school library. Participating NHS students were instructed to invite a staff member to attend and explain to the audience why he or she was summoned. A week prior to the event, Christine had approached me with her request for my presence. I must confess I was just a bit apprehensive at first; why not some other staff member? Still, my apprehension vanished and suddenly turned to seize the moment. We had known each other since she was a sixth-grade child prodigy, so it seemed a logical choice. An inner voice was telling me, *Who would want the custodian attending an honor society function?* My assessment was that perhaps the school needed someone available to clean up at the conclusion. Our occupational ilk doesn't exactly draw *oohs* and *aahs* from the general public. The bottom line: listen to your heart. She asked me and no one else, so I had to render a decision.

Several days prior to the event, Christine provided the itinerary for the evening, and, reassuringly, I was not required to wait on tables or muck out the kitchen. In addition, it would mean the world to this NHS inductee if I would attend. I decided to go with the flow and confirmed my intention to be present. Christine's brown eyes sparkled like ice crystals in the sun. So what if I embarrassed myself, it would not be the first time in my career. Furthermore, misfortune and humiliation merely purify man and prove his worth. In the end, I overcame any doubts overshadowing me. Emotionally, I prepared for what I hoped would be an evening to remember, especially for the sake of Christine.

To avoid upsetting my hostess, I made it a point to be punctual. I arrived sporting black slacks and a dress shirt apropos for the occasion. A staff member, familiar with my standard T-shirt and blue jeans attire commented, "My you clean up nicely!" The honor students were dressed to the nines and ardently waited on us hand and foot. Refreshments consisting of a cup of tea and chocolate decadent cake (topped with a sprig of mint) blended into a social hour. One of the most popular songs of the year, "Smooth," was dominating the rock and roll charts. Coincidentally, it also described how the evening's events progressed. When the time finally arrived for my introduction, Christine shared her reflections with everyone present. To this NHS student, I had become more than a custodian or her bus driver from years passed. I had evolved into the father she never knew, who was absent from her life. I was the one whom she could regard highly and obtain advice from.

I was thunderstruck beyond words with her kindness. I cherished that moment and realized that I must have done something right to become a positive role model for Christine. Ladies and gentlemen, this is what life is all about, what we strive for as school employees. Hard work plus dedication, the rewards are immeasurable.

One of the attendees at the social was Mr. Rigler, who spoke with me at length the following day. He was impressed by the comments Christine had made as much as I was. He delivered a thoughtful recap of the previous night's events, focusing on the highlights. "Father she never knew, huh? You must have influenced her life considerably." No one was more surprised than I was. I always considered my status as avuncular rather than fatherly. Whatever honorable image I portrayed, I have to believe this is the reason why we exist: we need to be positive role models.

Christine moved up in the ranks, becoming the NHS president, certainly a distinguished honor. She served her classmates proficiently while in office. Though I do not know where her future has taken her, I certainly wish Christine all the best in her life's endeavors.

SLITHER

The serenity that once enveloped the halls near the business education lab, was interrupted suddenly by a series of screams. Originating from inside a girls restroom, the unusual chorus fluctuated on the decibel scale. Bystanders watched, some perplexed, as girls scattered in different directions. Mr. Rigler and I tried to sort things out amid the pandemonium. What we stumbled upon was more indicative of a *Raiders of The Lost Ark* episode. Who would revive the role of Indiana Jones?

I had recently undergone the "new" custodian initiation process, so I was not sure what to expect. I soon discovered there are no two days that are identical, especially in a high school setting. If anyone knew what to anticipate, it was our business education instructor. Mrs. Sukamo ran a tight ship, held a black belt in martial arts and engaged a firm grip on anyone who would challenge her authority. She embodied nerves of steel to such a degree that no one dared harass her, not even the devil himself. She was a judicious, by the book educator, on her way to retirement. In some ways, she reminded me of Miss Lynch, the principal of Rydell High of "Grease" fame, but with an oriental flair. Consider that an august compliment.

One day, Mrs. Su (as she was known to the students) arrived at her classroom well in advance of her aspiring computer geeks. After unlocking the door, she entered and immediately relocked it to enjoy a few ephemeral moments of solitude. Mrs. Sukamo planned her day beforehand, as she realized her prep time preceding her first class tended to evaporate before her eyes. She hoped to squeeze out every possible minute in anticipation of the barrage of potential future computer programmers. She had no inkling she was about to become an unsuspecting yet obstinate victim of a practical joke.

Mrs. Su began her morning ritual by activating every student computer for the initial class about to arrive. Back in the 90s, a DSL modem was just a twinkle in its mother's eye. Logging onto the Internet using a dinosaur computer and primeval dial-up was a painfully slow process. These ancient computers' tortoise-like characteristics prompted you to query whether they operated on electricity or D batteries. Yet, that buzzing, screeching sound of the modems always reminded me of some feral animal giving birth, and when we had finally reached the browser home page, there was always a reason to celebrate.

On this particular morning, Mrs. Sukamo had settled into her desk, and then noticed something out of the corner of her eye moving across the floor in a bizarre manner. The average female staff member would have been intimidated. The majority of you who are squeamish at the mere sight of reptiles, would have high jumped or pole vaulted to the desk, and uttered some vile language at the top of your lungs. Not this crack-the-whip educator; she had a no-nonsense attitude. The prank failed to get much of a rise out of Mrs. Su, but it certainly captured her attention. The primary concern of this seasoned instructor was the incoming class, thus it was in her best interest to notify the office. Mrs. Sukamo faced a dilemma. How do you dispose of a slimy serpent?

The phone rang in Mr. Rigler's office as he sat at his desk with a serious pose; a pose we knew all too well. Considering this bizarre situation and the potential for complications to develop upon the arrival of students, our principal dashed to the computer class to assess the situation. Eliminating probable classroom disruption was half the battle. Separating fact from fiction, well, that was another story. He arrived at the computer lab in a New York minute, demonstrating he had not lost his youthful touch of incorporating his old school track capabilities. Rubbernecking students congregated in the hall, surmising what Mr. Rigler would encounter as he entered the classroom. The radio call was imminent.

It was a typical spring morning, with a generous portion of dairy air wafting through the countryside. A breeze would blow occasionally from the northwest, sending the offensive aroma onto the school campus. Equivalent to the odor of the run-of-the-mill mushroom plant, it stunk to high heaven the moment anyone exited the building. There was nothing we could do but complain, and complain we did.

The high school secretary's effort to deliver a message of impending danger fell flat when her words became interspersed with comedy. Is Mrs. Kinney serious? Maybe I was missing something. I needed to know what was going down and Mrs. K was showing her sense of humor, which she deemed necessary to maintain one's sanity in this environment. As Mr. Rigler entered the computer lab, he beheld Mrs. Sukamo holding a serpent, which she then delivered to our principal. A foot-long garden-variety garter snake was staring

Mr. Rigler in the face, complete with forked tongue. Our principal's countenance glowed like red hot charcoal. Mrs. Sukamo had made her point. An executive decision was rendered to transport the serpent to a reasonable and secure location (science lab) where it would be more productive.

I arrived at the classroom oblivious to the situation, as if I had been sailing in a fog. Mrs. Su gave me a guided tour of the room and called my attention to the blatant evidence the serpent had left behind. The dustpan was plausible as the perfect pooper-scooper, creating an easy cleanup. Just don't ask me about disposal. My memory escapes me. Meanwhile, our principal expressed an additional concern that sounded rational. What was the possibility that the serpent had relatives occupying the building?

His worst fears soon became a reality.

Girls bolted from a nearby restroom in terror, taking everyone by surprise and created some low-budget horror film ambience. Mr. Rigler and I timed it perfectly, arriving at the women's comfort station, where we discovered an audience displaying discomfort. We heard descriptions of swimming reptiles, varying in length and color, performing the breaststroke in the toilets. We concluded that somebody had concealed an unknown number of these guys in the building to terrify the female population. Mr. Rigler's scarlet face told the story. With no security cameras, we had no leads. An impromptu search was given and a rescue task force was organized comprising supplementary staff, including yours truly. In this limited edition of *Wild About Reptiles*, the staff zoomed in on the incident in the restroom itself. Some snakes seemed reluctant to be caught, whereas the intelligent ones slithered down the septic line. Eventually, they crossed over into the great abyss, never to be seen again.

Breathing sighs of relief and tranquility, everyone returned to their respective classrooms for the remainder of the day. The high school stood vigilant, uncertain whether the perpetrator(s) would be apprehended. The unforeseen appearance by members of the reptile family in the ladies room represented one of the premier pranks requiring my assistance. It also set the stage for future antics that the average student would never envision.

The Absentminded Custodian

One of my favorite classic TV shows of the past was the unpredictable *TV's Bloopers and Practical Jokes*. Numerous and repetitive takes by various actors were usually a hoot, because I could relate to their obliviousness while enjoying a good laugh at their expense. The same applies to *America's Funniest Home Videos*, though in a different tradition. This show provides an up close and personal glimpse of random family-oriented blunders.

So what about our own personal bloopers contributed to insomnia, ridiculous decisions, or other age-related factors? BF's, or brain farts are the perfect explanation for this lack of mental clarity. Perhaps we have pulled some nerdy stunts and preferred not to advertise—but that diminishes all the fun. Admitting that you really screwed up is a tall order and becomes a lesson learned the hard way.

I am sure some of you have an embarrassing moment you're just dying to share with the world. Save it for later, I would love to hear from you. In the meantime, allow me to provide you the 411 about myself and entertain you. I will weave my way through a fiasco that occurred during a high school fire drill and attempt to blame it on a lack of nocturnal slumber the night before. It played in as a contributing factor to the following sitcom.

A radio call from one of our secretaries informed me that it was the perfect morning for a fire drill. *My* perfect morning, by contrast, would encompass a fishing trip on the lake with temperatures in the sixties. "Will you be available for a drill at ten o'clock?" was the inquiry. I guessed that would work. I'd be over shortly to discuss the details. It wasn't as if I had a choice in the matter. The office ran the show, yet they needed me to show up. I guess I acted as the security blanket.

After what seemed like an eternity of consecutive days of living in a rain forest, we were finally blessed with a dry, though cloudy, day. I mentioned to Mrs. Kinney, "In the event of a real fire, you wouldn't have the option of a dry day would you?" While that would appear to be a no-brainer, their primary concerns were staff repercussions, e.g., wearing high heels and dress shoes on damp fields. A sticky collection of grass clippings from a recently mowed field would be tracked into the building, creating a skating-rink scenario. It meant job security, but, more importantly, created paperwork for the Safety Committee if I became a slacker.

Fire drills are analogous to having a cavity filled at the dentist. They are both procedures that inflict minor pain, but you always feel better once they are completed. Ten o'clock arrived, and I returned to the main office in a bit of a haze to retrieve the key that resets the alarm pull stations. There were nine keys on my key ring that looked identical. This one would be more accessible. It was my hope that everything would be free from encumbrances. A simultaneous drill conducted in four separate buildings required some extensive room checks. Staff would shout into each restroom doorway while the alarm pulsated. Occasionally, we would discover a student hiding. I walked out of the office and down the hall to locate a seldom-used pull station. Occasionally, one needs to remove freeloading arachnids that have set up camp for some time. After a brief communication between the individuals in charge, the green light was given to activate the switch. With the reset key safely tucked away, I pulled the alarm while a maintenance employee did likewise in another building.

The drill proceeded according to plan, with everyone evacuated on time and no casualties; that was the good news. I mention this with a hint of irony, because an unplanned drill on an icy morning may send you into a butt—scootin' boogie. After the evacuation, a head count was obtained and all students were accounted for, we presumed. The moment had arrived to summon the troupe back inside using the procedural three-bell ring. Everyone was returning to the high school when they encountered a major obstacle preventing them from entering. One absentminded custodian had not returned to the pull station to reset it; consequently, the alarm was triggered once again. Breaking all the rules pertaining to running in the halls, I sprinted like a clubfooted gazelle being persued by a fox all the way to the pull station and reached into my pocket for the key. No key. The principal pushed the reset code for the second time. To no avail; the alarm continued the ear bleeding, pulsating screech.

I remained calm, not reaching panic status yet, but it did cross my mind when I realized it was the worst possible time to lose my key. Dumbfounded and bordering on becoming brain-dead, I recalled that I carried a reset key on my key ring. Meanwhile, the high school secretary was on the radio, notifying me that our principal was once again unable to silence the alarm. I empathized with both of them as we advanced to the bonus round. I anxiously awaited an unruly crowd armed with torches and spears. I was also prepared to be blitzed with questions from the students (not to mention the staff) as they re-entered the building. It was time to compose a realistic answer to satisfy their curiosity and face the music.

An alarm-weary maintenance department was on the verge of going ballistic and becoming concerned that a technician needed to be notified. As for me, I was beginning to feel like a rash in the armpit. It was at that very moment the pull station was finally reset. Hence, we avoided another barrage of the deafening, pulsating alarms, and a spontaneous courtesy visit from Engine Number Nine. Everyone returned to his or her respective buildings. Thankfully, it remained dry outside, sparing any additional misery, and only a few students whined. I suppose they had reason to; they had been taking an exam at the time. When they returned to the classroom, they were told to retake it. Life can be so unfair.

I began to retrace my steps with high expectations of locating the missing key and salvaging a brutal morning. On a whim, I stuck my hand in my small change pocket. Well, what do you know . . . there it was. Some students walking by inquired, "Was there a malfunction in the fire drill?" I affirmed the query and chose not to keep the conversation open to discussion. In truth, I was the malfunction, if being asleep on the job qualifies. It was time to return to the high school office and pitch my story to what I hoped would be a sympathetic audience. They were.

Senior Pranks: The Crude Class

The source of the repulsive odor became evident as the bleacher seats in our high school gym began to gradually appear. As I held my thumb on the control button, all eyes focused on one specific bench. Similar to the malodorous surroundings at your local landfill, the stench was inescapable. That day I realized the typical gymnasium constitutes the perfect environment for a loathsome prank. No one was prepared for what lay ahead because it transcended his or her wildest imagination.

Let's face it, most of us find it entertaining when we are on the viewing end of a practical joke. When you suddenly become the focus of it, however, it is a completely different ballgame. Pranks are an inescapable part of our human nature. Yesterday's jests were simplistic and primarily amusing, and my own high school years are a perfect example. It was easy to obtain the locker combination of a classmate and very discreetly set the perfect booby trap. The secret to the success of this practical joke was contingent on timing and proper arrangement. Placing the largest book on top, a stack was designed to fall toward the student when the locker was opened, implementing a domino effect. Passersby stood back and watched in muted laughter. The reaction was priceless. Compare that to the intricate and occasionally malicious affairs that embody the post Generation Xers. You may have met some incognito as high school seniors.

May and June rank as the foremost months of spring. We finally get to dry out and harvest the moss that has been growing in our lawns since the past winter. In high school domains, however, those two months are omens of doom, particularly if you add a full moon to the picture. On those days, our administrators may beg/ pray for rain to quell a choice selection of scheming students from implementing their hidden agendas. On more than one occasion, some disconcerted members of our top brass have confided in me while venting their frustrations. Commencing about the first week in May, it becomes almost mandatory to patrol the various comfort stations, nooks, and crannies around campus as the staff prepares for the ultimate senior prank. Lastly, the month known for flowers and mothers was about to enter the pages of history. While it was a time to remember, it would become one I would rather forget.

It was seven straight up as I strolled into the teachers lounge to place my lunch inside our disgusting fridge, which had an interior that bore a resemblance to a specimen chiller in a biology lab. Scanning the internal compartments, I entertained second thoughts about leaving my brown bag in that environment. A hodgepodge of liquids had spilled over a period of years and mingled beneath the vegetable crisper to mold into an indistinguishable leather-like substance. Unknown specimens dwelled inside covered containers preparing to bear alien life forms. Of note was the fact that they had been in existence since Mrs. Jensen (our American history teacher) had retired and were primed for a mold spore count.

I turned my head in disgust, threw my lunch inside reluctantly, and closed the door. A plate of brownies on a nearby table conveyed a pleasant change of scenery. They seemed to broadcast a message: please sample me while you have the opportunity. I paused, gazing intently, and debated taking one. But since I was on a tight schedule, there wasn't a moment to spare or stop and taste test. They would have to wait. I decided to return later and inquire who had made this delectable treat.

Staff began to trickle in with high expectations, anticipating a low-key Friday following an exhausting week, but an unforeseen roadblock met a select minority. It was unfortunate. With their first encounter, they began to ask, "How do I open the door?" A few teachers entertained the thought that the locks had been altered, because their keys refused to enter the keyholes. Since the outside doors were the primary target, some notable staff members were left out in the elements. This meant Mrs. Borchers might be delayed from cutting those payroll checks on time. Thankfully, our maintenance staff (or Men of the Hour) arrived and cracked the case. They concluded that the keyholes had been deliberately superglued. It was time to fire up the heat-guns, which kept the guys scrambling. If you think those tools were red hot, you should have seen the expression on their faces.

First period was in progress when a surprisingly observant custodian wandered through the teachers lounge. The place was spotless, though somewhat disorganized, and, most importantly, some brownies had vanished, apparently eaten. "Hey ladies, who made those brownies?" I inquired as I entered the kitchen. Unfortunately, the cooks were mum on this subject, and it became increasingly evident they had no inkling where these eye-appealing goodies had originated. Anyone I spoke with was clueless regarding the identity of the evasive baker. What was particularly troubling was the fact that there was no note attached, giving us assurance they originated in Aunt Martha's kitchen. The mystery began to augment, and within the next hour, the remaining treats were confiscated, brought into the principal's office, and utilized as incriminating evidence. Rumors began to circulate that one ingredient in the brownies was derived from a popular plant. The administrators were dead-on in their assumption, and the cakes became exhibit A. Unfortunately, one of our teachers could not resist the temptation of chocolate (we do have our weaknesses) and consumed enough to alter his mental capabilities.

Yes, we had to hold someone accountable for this Schadenfreude, prompting a thorough investigation. The list of suspects was eventually condensed to a handful of students (of both sexes) known for pranking administrators. They were immediately summoned for questioning by the vice principal. Mrs. Winn's office began to shrink with the influx of bad company, perhaps resembling a police line for mug shots. Utilizing some five-O detective work and through the process of elimination, the staff narrowed the field down to one particular student. She carried the excess baggage in the form of her questionable reputation and providing too much information. It was reasonable to say she was like the thief who leaves all the fingerprints behind. Once the interrogations were completed, the men in blue paid a visit. She was promptly suspended and perhaps spent a few days in the Graybar Hotel (jail) for that incident. The remainder of the day became deathly quiet. It gave me a few moments to ponder what malevolent pranks the little darlins' were plotting for the coming week. Sigh!

Monday arrived (as it always does) like an express train. Both staff and students alike continued the countdown for the number of school days remaining. It was almost time to bring down the curtain on the current school year, with only a handful of activities still slated. Among them were May Week activities in Polynesian themes, featuring bright-hued skirts and ornate shirts. Relatively new to our school then, this event has become quite popular over the years. While the glamour of the event climaxed with the crowning of the island king, the glitter became the nuisance. I decided to chill out or "hang loose," as they say on the islands, while the Polynesian princesses showed their best dance moves on the gym floor Meanwhile, those prestigious awards for the super-jocks were still on tap. Coaches reserved the cafeteria almost daily for an evening of award plaques, preceded by Homestyle Buffet dinners. Trash cans always provide the evidence. The crude class would eventually exit into a world of hopes and dreams like those aspiring finalists on *American Idol.* While Ruben and Clay were fulfilling their desires, the senior class was preparing for theirs.

Mother Nature delivered a steady dose of Pacific Northwest drizzle, permeating the atmosphere. It was the equivalent of standing adjacent to a produce mister in a supermarket when it is suddenly activated. It provided the appropriate meaning to a bad hair day. I expected much more from the month of flowers than that gloomy environment. It has often been said that summer does not arrive until July 5th, with rare exceptions. Physical education and body development classes were held inside that day, and students complained of foul odors. No surprise here. Mix thirty-some bodies exuding fluids while exercising in a gym that feels like a sauna—you're talking some pretty ripe conditions. When the radio call advised me to probe and identify a particularly rank aroma, I had no difficulty zeroing in on the source. While pinching their nostrils, some students drew attention to the bleachers as the bulls eye for this odious prank. The painfully slow process of waiting for the bleachers to separate was like watching a flower bud open. All eyes were glued to the seats, and the origin of that wretched smell began to manifest itself in the form of fish entrails. Thankfully, it was an effortless cleanup, but its simplicity concerned me. A couple students divulged what they knew, and I began to feel queasy at the thought of it. This was just a warm-up for the main event. It was time to prepare for the worst.

Cautiously, I walked up the steps to the upper level of the gym as the stench grew stronger and almost intolerable. Some students pointed to two overhead heaters and I reflected, *Certainly, these kids couldn't toss fish guts that high, could they?* Never underestimate the determination of a senior when he or she is committed to a prank. Locating a ladder capable of reaching the top of the heating unit was a challenge. Mr. Rossitto, our AG instructor, located a twelve footer in his barn, giving me enough height for a visual. First, he had to extricate the owl perched at the top. Mr. Rossitto appreciated the prompt return of all items borrowed—you did not want to mess with the Enforcer.

My theory was on the money, as predicted. Perched on top and cooked to perfection were two fish fillets. It was one more reason why I carried a putty knife in my back pocket; it performed as effectively as a spatula. The audience below cheered briefly before additional discouraging words came crashing in my direction from ground level. A rolled-up wrestling mat lying idle on the floor stunk to high heaven and presented itself as the centerpiece of attraction. With an inquisitive crowd gathered, my chances of evading this predicament were hopeless. They left me no choice but to roll out the mat, examine the contents, and solve any mysteries contained therein.

Curiosity finally got the better of two freshmen boys, who volunteered their services and were ready to assist me at a moments notice. The three of us had our hands full attempting to unravel this massive piece of athletic equipment, albeit discreetly, as we choked and gagged along the way. For every foot that was revealed, their inquisitive brain cells became more stimulated. Their faces displayed that (reality show)*Fear Factor* look. Eventually, we arrived at the end to a sight so revolting, it brought new meaning to the word "putrid." Fish heads, hidden during the previous week, had become flyblown. I've said enough. I might add, however, that it was the perfect environment, considering the number of days they were left undisturbed. Though the mat was a perfect candidate for the burn pile, this would have crippled our wrestling coach's budget. Therefore, I had to come up with a plan B.

The key ingredients to a less-than-miraculous renovation were two quarts of disinfectant and a body D workout. By retaining my services, the wrestling program saved some serious *dinero* that day, and the district came out smelling like a rose. Can't say the same about the mat. Furthermore, we never did divulge to our next opponents what organisms had been living on the mat. As repugnant as this prank was, the important fact remained: nothing was damaged. That has to say something. Nevertheless, I was ready for that day to be over, but one project still remained on the docket: lunch cleanup.

The garbage was mounting at the blink of an eye due in part to a mounting Styrofoam tray collection. The next lunch featured the worst offenders from the high school. I labeled their method "trash and dash." They would wait until my back was turned, then scamper like scared rabbits, leaving an assortment of odds and ends. Those insolent students turned a deaf ear to my pronouncement, "Hey, your momma doesn't work here, pick up your tray." I wasted my breath on an audience with selective hearing.

Our science teacher, Mr. Bauer, ventured through an assemblage of students, who nearly prohibited his forward progression to the condiment bar. Subsequent to his choice of dressing, I drew attention to wannabe artists and sculptors, who left their creations to public viewing. Apples, pierced and decorated with plastic forks, bore an uncanny resemblance to Old Sol, while bananas appeared to be growing appendages. Anything left to the imagination was the norm, and what a waste at bell time. Other miscreants, bored with school lunches, thought it would be cute to set a trap for an unsuspecting janitor. Carefully, I reached for an empty tray containing only a milk carton. As fate would have it, the slightly tilted, open carton fell toward me, coating my jeans with a generous dose of vitamin D. Laundering was pending, otherwise I wouldn't be fun to be around by days end.

The crime scene (as I referred to it) nearly reached a point of intimidation. Add to that a bit of concern that no assistance would arrive. It appeared I would be staying late once again. It was time to call home and give the drudgery report. My liberation finally occurred, however, when the entertaining work skills class exploded on the scene like a nervous ball of energy. While their work etiquette was a little off-the-wall, they managed to complete the job in their time slot. I admired the teaching staff, because it required an extraordinary group of individuals to run this hyperactive crew. They deserved a medal at the very least for retaining their sanity as they dealt with a daily dose of uncorked energy. And me? I was ready for the departure of this Class.

LUNCH OR BURNT OFFERINGS?

If a dense haze has settled within the confines of a high school home economics class, I can speculate that one of two situations has transpired. Either Evergreen Valley High is about to go up in flames and evacuation is imminent, or cooking class is in progress.

Perhaps this is a degree of exaggeration, but the facts speak for themselves. We have seen the smoke, it goes with the program, and we know the drill. At least once a week, an aroma wafts down the hall, enticing students like a ravenous pack of wolves in search of a free meal. For the dreamers, it is visions of handouts of Macho Burritos or General Tsao's Chicken. The district maintains a closed campus policy, so this is the student's golden hour to imitate their restaurant chain of choice. Everyone knows the source of that mesmerizing odor originates inside the foods room, where future chefs and cooks are created and nurtured.

RSVPs were hand-delivered to a small cluster of high school staff chosen at random to attend a future luncheon. Our benevolent principal, Mr. Rigler, and I were part of the muster and graciously accepted. Some invited guests, like Mr. Bixby, our counselor, were as excited as little kids anticipating Christmas. For others, it was just another day, but keep the Tums handy. Facial expressions told the true story.

Comparable to a quaint eatery, it appeared our hosts were thrilled with our presence. We were waited on like visiting dignitaries and shared tales of previous luncheon encounters. I think we qualified as professional food testers and shared little concern about the repast we were about to consume. Our buoyant foods teacher, Mrs. Vincente, took extraordinary measures and assured us that all preparations were palatable. Being a perfectionist, Mrs. V, with her infectious chuckle, approved all menu items right down to the last snicker doodle.

Back in the day, our priorities were divergent, especially during my high school cooking class. There was far greater emphasis on getting an A, as opposed to getting salmonella. I doubt if it ever crossed our minds, because during that time food handling and food poisoning were seldom discussed issues. Our emphasis was primarily focused on presentation, not preservation.

My high school home economics group, wielding some clout, ventured to invite the principal to dine with us, beating out the competition. We served a delectable three—course home-style meal, complete with dessert, that garnered some attention. The downside was having little appetite, knowing that Mr. Fletcher was dining at our table. What if he despised our lunch and/or divulged his experience to other staff members? I stayed up half the night for no reason. In the end, the luncheon was a success, and the principal enjoyed his meal. Well, at least that is what he related to us. Mrs. Fairfield, our home economics teacher was so impressed, she gave everyone an A.

Fast forward to the 90s where the tables are turned and I became the evaluating diner. Mrs. Vincente's crew of amateur cooks was under pressure, like those culinary chefs on Food Network's *Chopped*. As they began concocting the attending staff's lunch, the crackle and the sizzle amplified with the intense cooking. We became apprehensive for good reason, because the entrées were beginning to resemble those biblical burnt offerings. Flaming dishes can also attract attention for both the right and wrong reasons. Although the cooking class showed the best of intentions, some neglected to lower the heat at the proper moment. As a result, Hell's Kitchen was born.

A hungering staff waited anxiously for the Mexican repast, while the foods room was acquiring a pool hall's haze. I had to wonder how long it would take for the smoke detector to activate before asphyxiation kicked in. It failed to respond, leaving little room for doubt that replacement was imminent. Invited guests became concerned as the room began filling with smoke at an alarming rate. Everyone began inching toward the direction of a glass door leading to a veranda, the only outside source of ventilation. Breathing gradually grew labored as remaining staff and students bolted to the source of air, while someone decided to open the classroom door to the hallway. A wall of smoke gushed into the hall, attracting students, while others fled the foods room. With flames nonexistent, it made the situation appear to be more of a grand illusion. The exhaust fans were the last resort, but eventually that too became a nuisance. One imitated a limping 747 with a defective propeller.

Inside the home ec. class, the valiant Mrs. Vincente was handling the cooking catastrophe better than a cooking show reject. The word "agitated" was not part of this teacher's diction, and she shifted into backup mode. First, Mrs. V sent one student to the office to have her contacts cleaned. Poor Molly experienced a "Smoke Gets in Your Eyes" vision dilemma. The remaining students, save the sick and the lame, regrouped for plan B. In less time than it takes to say "fire up the barbie" the skillets were hot, and we had some serious cooking going on. We regained our appetites and sense of smell while the new batch of fajitas was looking more hopeful. Who cared if we smelled as if we had just returned from firefighting? It would be a topic for discussion at the next luncheon. In the end, we concluded with a two-for-one deal, with staff in agreement. Nothing like a little drama on the side. A free and extended lunch makes a pretty good bang for the buck.

An eerie, deathly quiet came over us after everyone dispersed: no calls, no crises, nothing. The first lunch was completed, now it was time for the high school, arriving like a den of bears following hibernation. Just a few more tables to clean, and I'd beat the rush. Perish the thought.

The first call came in. The foods room needed my presence again; some of the sinks were plugged. I arrived with plunger in hand only to discover vegetables were washed down the drain. This had to be a female issue. It appeared there was a certain degree of difficulty depositing leftover food in the trash. Next question, where were the sink strainers? Then another call came in, the report of a plugged toilet in the boys' room in our agricultural building. That could be a ten-minute job. But wait, a third call came over the radio. Now, there was a sticky liquid spill in the cafeteria. Can't one of the lunch monitors wipe the floor? Where is everybody? I could have gone off the deep end, but I held it together. It was now time to clone myself.

WHERE DID YOU LEAVE
THE CAR KEY?

Breaking into and entering a vehicle are likely to bring handcuffs slapped on your wrists and expeditious vacation time in Graybar Hotel if apprehended. It becomes lawful, however, when accomplished by a qualified school maintenance employee; permission granted of course. One prevalent method of entry is using a device commonly known in the locksmith and towing professions as a "slim jim." The odds are usually two to one in my favor when this amazing little invention is properly applied, provided the internal locking mechanism can be located.

The preferred option, with a 99.9 percent accuracy rate, is the indisputable spare key. How many students will ponder that fact? In my experience, history tends to indicate zero, the goose egg, because the word "foresight" is not contained in their vocabulary. I realize those using keys containing microchips may require a short term loan, but they're as good as insurance. Prior experience tends to show that unless the parents are enrolled in a roadside service plan, they are likely to be set back a few Benjamins when D-Day arrives.

First, there was Chelsea, a vibrant high school junior, requesting I use forced entry to get into her late—model Jetta. This VW just happened to be displaying the anti-theft logo. Adding insult to injury, her spare key was in Mom's possession at the time, which presented another quandary. I asked Chelsea, "Why don't you call Mom and have her bring the key?" It's simple. The red head driver shrugged her shoulders and let out a deep sigh, "She's in Colorado" (a two-day drive). We had to look on the positive side. With the absence of a car key, Chelsea was less likely to be involved in a fender bender.

I am always amazed at the collection of late-model street rods that occupy our school parking lot. What is more surprising is the number of female students driving a set of wheels fresh off the car lot. I must be in the wrong business. The newer the vehicle, the greater the challenge to hone your break in skills. All the sophisticated electronic gadgetry simply adds to the misery. In a face-to-grille encounter with a Ford Shelby GT-500, I deemed it imperative that I contact a parent or guardian first before I rearranged the wiring. For those who desire a daily workout, try using a slim jim on a Cadillac. The die-hards still drive those Sherman tanks and gas hogs for a reason. Do not let the older models fool you. An 80s Caddy maintains maximum illegal-entry protection based on previous break-in attempts.

One of my pet peeves is the student who waits until the dismissal bell before realizing his or her key was left on the seat or in the ignition. Some prudence would have given all parties involved ample time to prepare for this momentous event. Anyway, who has time to reflect on the absence of a car key when "crucial" text messages must be delivered? Everyone has his or her priorities. With no spare available within a ten-mile radius, what was once considered a nuisance gradually evolved into a state of anxiety. The possibility this teenage driver would arrive at work tardy had become a reality. Never mind that the wind chill has reduced the mercury to single digits and numbness in my fingers has progressed to the early stages of frostbite.

Mr. Bartel was crossing the parking lot at that moment and arrived to offer assistance. This slender, well-intentioned staff member perceived that I had been working meticulously and without success, trying to unlock a student's vehicle. He came up to me and said, "Why don't you let me have a crack at it?" I tell him, "Sure, go for it." What could he possibly do that would accelerate my futile attempt? Employing no effort whatsoever, he uses my slim jim and accomplishes the feat in less than a minute, while I've burned at least ten. So much for my ninja skills that day. I concluded that any potential employment as a locksmith or professional burglar was as promising as lowering the national debt.

Students may take most of the credit, but there are exceptions. Enter Mr. Wolfer, a preoccupied English teacher, whose large wire rimmed glasses, nestled at the end of his long nose. It was inconceivable this man had misplaced (for lack of a better word) his ignition key, presenting yet another fascinating observation of high school life. Mr. Wolfer was reasonably certain it remained somewhere in his vehicle, and contacting the nearest towing company was out of the question. Obviously, they charge for service calls and I do not. With a lot on my plate, my time must be worth an ounce of something. Mr. Wolfer assured me that the key was resting on the seat or somewhere in the vehicle, despite a lack of visual evidence. Cynicism began to creep into the picture, and I embarked on a questionable procedure that had all the earmarks of a lost cause.

The gales of December greeted me prior to my arrival at the pop-a-lock festivities. It didn't seem to matter which direction I moved, for I was constantly battered by a tenacious blast in my face, nearly immobilizing my body. With the finesse of a surgeon, I slid the slim jim alongside the window and inside the door near the handle.

At some point, I met resistance, and there was still no word from the teacher as the day reached the eleventh hour. Eventually, I retracted that invaluable break-in tool, as it appeared to have disconnected a much needed wire. Only minutes later, word arrived that Mr. Wolfer had found the ignition key in his classroom. I'm sure there was a logical explanation, but one never materialized. I was warned about the intricacies of late-model vehicles and their pitfalls. While there was no need to summon a towing service, placing a call for the nearest auto mechanic was not out of the question.

Thankfully, Mr. Wolfer's troubles were resolved minus any wiring snafus. Mine however, were about to escalate into the unexpected. I had recently been assigned yet one more duty, due to the absence of our reliable laundress. Every school has one, right? Always taking the reins of a laundry room in constant disarray, Carrie was the go-to gal. She was a woman for all seasons. From baseball to football, she appeased every coach, if that was possible. But retirements are inevitable and life can change in a flash. An aging body frame has a tendency to reduce mobility and accelerate those long awaited pension checks.

The baton was passed down to me, and I added one more job to my roster. I shared no excitement in this new opportunity, but felt a sense of satisfaction knowing I could accomplish what he did. Now, instead of washing only my crap once a week, I had to add the kitchen laundry into the mix. After I placed the assorted items into a black plastic bag, a staff member passed by me in the hall and made the Santa connection. Imagine the look on kids faces at Christmas when opening their presents.

The laundry room was built at the end of a tunnel vaguely resembling a bomb shelter. Perhaps it was a safe place to hide in a storm, but you'd be a sitting duck in an earthquake. The entry door required an access code, but failed to recognize the series of numbers I input. "When all else fails, use the master key," I always say. The door opened with much effort to a display that had all the earmarks of a secondhand store. Clothing from nearly every major sport was represented inside, such as basketball trunks, spandex, volleyball jerseys, football paraphernalia—you get the picture. My cleaning supplies became buried in the rubble, and I didn't know who to blame.

Everyone needs a little music to work by, so "Dirty Laundry" was a dead ringer. Hopefully that would produce a motivation factor. It didn't, but it was like the key in the ignition. The pre-soak items were still soaking and could go another day. I shoveled the jerseys into the washer, hit the button, and the machine took over. The only thing that could dig me out of this mess was a backhoe. At that point, it was time to evacuate, catch my breath, and return in an hour. As usual, everything was contingent upon a radio call tug-of-war between the secretaries. Like clockwork, you could set your watch for noon. Something was going to happen.

MORE SENIOR PRANKS: THE CLASS OF AMAZEMENT AND WIT

Like those foreboding scientists predicting the next major earthquake, I knew something was going to happen; I just didn't know what or when. Unlike those scientific scholars, there was minimal anxiety in my mind, reflecting more of a peaceful apprehension. In a direct communiqué, I was notified I would witness "elements of amazement and wit" on behalf of the senior class. I received that information courtesy of an informant. I had to keep up with the real world too. Could the graduates produce their own version of the Amazing Kreskin? Given the imagination and flair they possessed, staff had no doubts.

Serena Harris and Courtney Palmer were the vocal wonders among our seniors and could have been contestants on any of today's reality competition shows. Courtney's exuberance and outgoing personality were two of her many qualities that radiated among those she met. Serena's vocal capabilities immediately propelled her into the national spotlight as an entertainer. If I requested information or needed to overcome the dark elements of the week, both were inspiring.

No one could underestimate the mindset of these seniors and what they were capable of doing. At some point I heard the prank described as hilarious. Better the component of humor than a moment of exasperation. Wary administrators received forewarnings, and while information conveyed may have settled their nerves, shadows were cast on the encroaching year's end. This senior class would not break their code of silence regarding their pranks and remained mum to its fulfillment. Regardless how minimal the damage probabilities might have been, it was a safe bet I would be involved in some aspect of the aftermath.

As it concluded, May was a month of ambiguities for many potential graduates. For some, it meant passing or failing one class, which would determine whether a student would receive his or her certificate of distinction. As our high school secretaries were busy filing the needed paperwork for each student, alterations were made hourly. Right up to the day before the ceremony, seniors were informed whether they would parade across the stage or become an audience viewer. There was ample reserved seating for the charlatans who tried to milk the system. And as always, there were the procrastinators, dreaming of a miraculous eleventh-hour drive-thru diploma service.

Unlike previous graduations, this forthcoming commencement would present an aura of uniqueness, which I'd eventually discover. It would become an unprecedented moment in my custodial career as well as my life. A considerable amount of brainstorming by the seniors was instrumental in acquiring a modification in the graduation ceremony. As was tradition, the graduating class voted for the instructors/staff members of their choice to announce the names at graduation. Among this year's staff picks from the senior class, the majority requested their custodian.

Mrs. Kinney called me to the office and without hesitation, dropped a bombshell on me. She announced that I was one of the finalists chosen to present diplomas for this graduating class. Competent and qualified were two adjectives that burned in my mind. Public speaking wasn't prominent on my bucket list; in fact, it didn't make the list, period. I needed to mull it over for a few days. Then I listened to Mrs. Kinney and Mrs. La Voie, our secretaries, implore, "You have to do it for us Dan. You can represent the classified staff." While it was a big deal for them, I had to consider another factor: disappointing the seniors.

Anyway, nothing was signed in blood. It was not long before the student council discovered a technicality that would bar me from making an appearance. For the senior class officers, it was the equivalent of filing a proceeding through an appeals court. What could I do, but allow the jury to convene and wait for the verdict to be delivered. I was beginning to feel as though I was the poster child for the classified staff, becoming a victim of the system. I felt like the defendant at his trial, waiting for his attorney to take the stand. Life had to go on. There were more pressing matters to deal with, i.e., removing a hacky sack off the roof, along with the shoe that put it there.

Finally, the gavel came down against the plaintiff(s), objection overruled. This left one unanswered question, why the uproar? Well, according to tradition, only teaching staff have read names at graduation; but, that was about to change. Whatever intervention the Class of Amazement used, it worked. The senior officers returned, and I delivered a formidable praise of the procedure. Suddenly the barricades were removed. Then I received confirmation that I could indeed read names at their graduation and heard a resounding "yes." The student council members beamed as if they had won a settlement. The hard fought battle was over.

Now it was up to me. The senior officers had done their part. It was the chance of a lifetime to prove to our graduates, the staff, and the audience at large that I could step into the same shoes as our educators.

Without exception, it was considered an honor to be nominated. My public address background was minimal, limited to a couple of brief moments behind a church pulpit before a modest audience. Like the surfer waiting for the perfect wave to mount, the anticipation intensified. The point in time finally arrived when a contingent of student body officers reintroduced the question: would you like to read names at graduation? Without hesitation, I responded with an emphatic "yes." Suddenly, a pair of high school secretaries started squealing, like two little girls in a candy store.

Nathan Sims was one of our juniors who began to reverberate the sentiments of the senior class. His facial features, shoulder-length hair and guitar talents, were indicative of the 60's. One glance during a band session and you had to wonder, could he have played lead guitar for the "Doors." It was also his trademark to utter "slanguage," or jargon that would make you cringe in public. Whenever he increased his speaking volume, it was the equivalent of a megaphone at close range. One would seek either the nearest exit doors or ear plugs to avoid embarrassment if nothing else. "Holy ___ Dan the Man, are you reading names at graduation?" "Yes, I believe so." "Crap, that's awesome man." Then he rambled off a comparison between me and some famous figure like Gandhi.

Thanks for the accolade Nathan—it was imperative that you greet him by his complete first name, no abbreviations. Anything less and you were subject to a brief rant—but I am only the custodian.

Fast forward to June, where graduations tend to sneak up on you, as April 15th does to a tax accountant. Efforts were underway to transform a *ginormous* hollow building into a commencement facility of prodigious grandeur, a feat in itself. To think I once attended concerts in this same structure still amazes me. A mandatory practice session was held to iron out the wrinkles and keep the foot traffic flowing. The computer geeks prepared their ever-popular slide presentation, banking on a program that would run like clockwork.

So what if it didn't? Any mistakes would be part of the show, and the show must go on.

Straight up eight and time to rock and roll. The moment had finally arrived. With great honor, I paraded in line amongst the teaching staff to the continuous sound of pomp and circumstance. Following on our heels were the graduates displaying their glorious regalia accompanied by a contingency of horn blowers. Past tradition allowed them to adorn their caps, where often creativeness could go to extremes. Although the weather outside was unseasonably nippy, inside the heater was cranking out those BTUs, and I was progressively drowning in excessive diaphoresis. Sure, two-hour commencements are run of the mill, with exception: when you are one of the lectors, time is suspended.

As I watched the various photographs of students in both their senior and elementary poses projected on the wall, it brought back memories of my daughter's graduation some years earlier. It also gave me a moment to pause and reflect, realizing that in less than a year she would repeat the ceremony in college, and once again, I would witness a proud and historic moment. Where did the time go? I tried to keep my mind focused, knowing that in a short period diplomas would be distributed.

An extraordinary senior took the stage via a wheelchair lift to not only receive a diploma but also prove to the world that nothing would hold her back. She was Miss Independent. This brilliant, witty and upbeat 12th grader with a jet-black pixie hairstyle imparted upon us her genuinely infectious smile. Jenny was a favorite among staff and students and became a motivator for this class. Once, she wowed me with her talented computer skills. Someday, Jenny may be programming for the big boys.

The progression of the commencement ceremony was incessant, which was most appreciated by both the staff and audience. Viewing the ceremony from the balcony seats was the equivalent of spending two hours in Louisiana in the middle of August. For the previous years, it was as close as I could get. Now row four was approaching the halfway point when I made my way to the stage awaiting my cue. A little nudge would have been nice, or perhaps some words of wisdom, for instance "stuttering is not an option." Anyway, there was no time to dwell; it was showtime.

Once on stage, I approached the podium guardedly, due to the stage lights beaming in my face. I could almost feel the heat. I took every precaution to make sure I would remain incident free. One faux pas and I'd be memorable for the wrong reasons. Though I had the list of names before me, my attempt to read them was squelched by a thunderous applause. The senior class erupted into a loud cheering section reminiscent of a rock concert. I thanked the receptive audience in a punctuating delivery before they finally relented.

Thanks to a unique method of speech preparation I had stumbled across, any apprehension I might have had, vanished before the gargantuan and frenzied crowd. Interspersed throughout this rollicking audience were the sounds of noisemakers and party favors. These, I realized, were the icebreaker I needed. Like a seasoned politician giving his polished acceptance speech, I nailed it when it came to pronunciations, and felt a sense of accomplishment. Furthermore, my voice boomed over the microphone. Returning to my seat, I was greeted with handshakes and high fives along the route. And it didn't stop there.

The following day, more plaudits continued to pour in from all directions. Both staff and students recognized a historical moment in the annals of Evergreen Valley High School graduation. Even the local media carried highlights of my time at the podium, which simply added icing on the cake. It was a tough pill to swallow for the skeptics and naysayers. Meanwhile, the seniors were languishing in the comfort of their beds after the all-night festivities, with the exception of a few defectors who carried out their own agenda. The time had finally arrived for the diehard seniors to perform. This class, more than any prior did not want to disappoint us.

It was Monday morning when school personnel stumbled onto a deluge of antics. Tennis balls were strewn about the cafeteria floor, creating a difficult if not impossible walking environment. Someone had an unlimited cash flow. Lunch tables in the commons were interlaced with multicolored streamers, creating a rainbow effect. Zip ties decorated every locker handle in the freshman hall. This required an amassment of volunteers armed with pliers before any students could stash their prized possessions. Of course the girls sighed, since they could not access their personal mirrors to apply make-up and lipstick. Each restroom mirror displayed a message of endearment, conveniently written with tempura paints. Maybe they were thinking of me, because the cleanup was minimal. The odor of a cheap toilet spray permeated the hallway.

Perhaps the best prank of all was the method used by the seniors to achieve this stunt and elude the cameras. Each graduate was asked to provide a photo of their favorite country or rock star. The photos were transformed into posters, which were placed directly in front of each camera by students wearing hoodies. When the camera tapes were reviewed, the students involved were unrecognizable; only the entertainers images could be seen. Those "elements of amazement and wit" had finally transpired. And ingenious they were. Even today, evidence of this elusive class remains. Inscribed on a poster are the names of all the graduates and the words "the class of Amazement rules." The poster has been stored away for possible presentation at a future reunion.

Life goes on and the world continues to evolve around the seniors, as it always will. Many pranksters have come and gone, being replaced by yet another bold and brazen species. In a strange, twisted way, it is their rite of passage. Every year will yield its share of those who seek recognition. Whether popular or infamous, they will leave a legacy, as will every future graduating class. A future class is on the horizon that is likely to have every staff member asking, "How did they do that? It's impossible."

I peruse the many faces of yesterday displayed in a stack of annuals resting idly on the shelves collecting dust. As I look at our school, I visualize those who have come and gone. Then I walk through the clutter-free halls and see my reflection in the freshly-waxed floors, rejuvenated bathroom mirrors, and in the eyes of the students filled with expectations.

ABOUT THE AUTHOR

Daniel D. Johnson is a Head Custodian for a rural school district in Oregon. The author is also a freelance writer with articles published in print and online. A native South Dakotan, he resides with his wife and a high-strung bichon mix.

Slang Glossary

Benjamins	100 dollar bills
Dinero	Spanish for money
411	Information
Graybar Hotel	Jail
Homies	Friends
Motormouth syndrome	Someone who talks incessantly and doesn't realize it
OMG	Oh my gosh!
Slanguage	Slang language
Sup?	Abbreviation for What's Up?
TMI	Too much information
University of Clueless	The alternative to higher education if you can't make wise decisions

Made in the USA
Las Vegas, NV
05 October 2021